The Mediator

HEAVEN TO EARTH, GOD TO MAN

JACK REHILL

KINGDOM
BOOK ENDEAVORS

Dedication

This book is dedicated to our Harvest Church
family in Trucksville, Pennsylvania, with whom
we have been a family for the past 29 years,
through ups and downs, triumphs and tragedies,
successes and failures, times of peace and
times of conflict. Nevertheless, through it all,
the God and Father of our Lord and
Savior Jesus Christ, by the power of
the Holy Spirit, has helped us to,
as Ephesians 4:2–3 says,

*"Be completely humble, gentle, and patient,
bearing with one another in love, and straining
every nerve to maintain the unity of the
Spirit in the bond of peace."*

Acknowledgments

I am most grateful for the support of my wife,
Patricia, who has been by my side for 54 years.
She is a champion of the truth, and I can always count
on her opinions and suggestions, which are never
sugarcoated to tell me what I want to hear,
but straightforward to tell me what I need to hear,
and she is usually right.

I would also like to acknowledge and thank
our son-in-law, Mason, for his skill and help
in the front and back cover design of this book,
which he somehow seems to graciously fit into
his own busy schedule of speaking and writing.

Lastly, I would like to acknowledge and I'm grateful
for the addition of a third grandchild,
Jeffrey Benjamin, born to our son-in-law, Mason, and
daughter Johanna, who also has brought great joy
to our lives along with his cousins, Lyla and Claudia.

Table of Contents

Introduction

Have you ever noticed that the Bible ends the way it begins? God created the heavens and the earth and everything in them. He created man in His own likeness and image out of the dust of the earth. Then God decided that it wasn't good for the man to be alone. So, He took the man and put him into a deep sleep and took his side and created a woman for him and brought her to the man to be his wife. The man, Adam, declares in Genesis 2:23,

> "This is now bone of my bones
> And flesh of my flesh;
> She shall be called Woman,
> Because she was taken out of Man."

Genesis 2:8 says, "The Lord God planted a garden eastward in Eden, and there he put the man whom he had formed." The Bible goes on to say that God provided trees to eat from, rivers to drink from; essentially everything they would ever need. They would not have to work for it, they would only have to care for what God had created for them.

Genesis 2:15 says, "Then the LORD God took the man and put him in the garden of Eden to tend and keep it." God not only did all of this for the man and his wife, but He, Himself, intended to live with them in that garden forever.

However, in Genesis 2:16–17, we read that God gave the man just one commandment: "Of every tree of the garden, you may freely eat [In other words, help yourself!], but of the tree of the knowledge of good and evil you shall not eat, for in the day that you eat of it you shall surely die."

Notice that it says, "for in the day that you eat of it." It doesn't say, "*if* you eat of it." I personally believe that God knew they were going to fail to keep that command. I base that opinion on Revelation 13:8, which refers to the Lord Jesus as the "Lamb slain from the foundation of the world." Why would God have a lamb slain from the foundation of the world if He thought they were going to obey His command?

The world we live in today is not the world that God originally intended. How many times have we heard people say, "If God is such a good God, if He is such a loving God, why does He allow pain and suffering and sickness and tragedy?"

Well, first of all, He allows it because He "allowed" the man and the woman He created after His own image and likeness to have a will as He does. He gave them the power to choose. There would be no coercion on His part. If that were the case, He could've just made us all robots and programmed us according to His will. However, He chose to make us so that He could love us and so that we could choose to love Him.

The power to choose was exclusive to mankind. None of the rest of the living beings that God created possessed this power—none of the beasts of the earth, the fish of the sea, or the birds of the air. Only the man and the woman that God created after His own image and likeness. This is so significant because it means we live and die by the choices we make. One decision can change the course of my whole life. One decision can change the course of history. One choice—the choice to disobey the command of God—caused the fall of all the rest of humanity that came after Adam and Eve. The moment they made that decision, they brought death into everything that God had created.

However, the apostle Paul declares great news in Romans 5:19, letting us know that the choice of the first Adam was reversed by the choice of the last Adam, Jesus, the Mediator.

It was always God's desire that the man and woman He created would freely exercise their will in conformity to His will. But they chose not to do that with the help of the serpent, Satan, who deceived them into thinking they could be their own gods.

And so, they passed on that disobedient nature to the rest of humanity to live according to our own will and fleshly desires. Galatians 5 refers to it as "the sinful nature" in the Amplified Bible.

All of us are born with a sinful nature. There was only one who was not born with a sinful nature, the Mediator, the spotless, sinless, Son of God—Jesus the Christ. The One who said in John 6:38, "For I have come down from heaven, not to do My own will, but the will of Him who sent Me."

God's original plan was for the man and woman He created to obey His command. He never wanted them to be the vessel through which sin, sorrow, grief, pain, and ultimately death would spoil His creation.

It was never God's intent that humanity would be separated from Him, nor heaven separated from earth, nor mankind separated from one another through death.

The entire theme of the Bible is bringing heaven back to earth, man back to God, and mankind back to eternal life. It is how Genesis begins and how the book of Revelation ends, with a long detour in between.

In order for God's ultimate plan of restoration to be executed, it had to be mediated. And in order for it to be mediated, there had to be a mediator. 1 Timothy 2:5 says, "For there is one God and one Mediator between God and men, the Man Christ Jesus."

What is the role of a mediator? To bring parties together who have been separated by conflict. A mediator is a go-between to help settle conflict and bring the parties back together. When Adam and Eve disobeyed the command of God and ate from the Tree of the Knowledge of Good and Evil they brought about irresolvable, irreconcilable conflict between God and mankind. He had warned them that the day they ate from it they would die. There would eventually be an end to their days upon the earth. But much worse than that, there would be an immediate separation from the presence of the One who made them, provided for them, and watched over them. And there would be nothing they could do to reverse it.

Furthermore, not only would they suffer the curse of being forever separated from the presence of God, but that curse would be passed on to every successive generation. All of humanity would be forever separated from God. All of heaven and everything heavenly, joyful, peaceful, and loving would be forever separated from the earth. All of humanity would be forever separated from one another through death, and all because of one choice of one man and one woman. The only hope was for a mediator to step in and bring mankind back to God, heaven back to earth, and humanity back to one another.

Where would such a mediator come from? It could not be anyone on earth. Everyone on earth was under the same curse. It could only be someone from heaven, someone who wasn't under the curse of separation from God. It could only be the only begotten Son of God coming down from heaven, Jesus. He would have to die to pay the penalty for Adam's failure.

Christ Jesus, the Mediator, mediated the restoration of mankind to God, earth to heaven, and death to life, with His loving willingness to pay the penalty of death for Adam's sinful disobedience to the command of God. And then to forever release us from the power of sin with the power of His resurrection.

John 3:16, a very familiar portion of scripture, says, "For God so loved the world that He gave His only begotten Son [as the Mediator], that whoever believes in Him should not perish [be forever separated from God] but have [be restored to] everlasting life." And we might add, "together with all those who have believed."

Chapter One

The Presence of the Lord

*I*t has always been God's intent to dwell with the people He created right from the very beginning of creation. That is why He made the heavens and the earth and everything in them, to be a dwelling place for the man and the woman He created and to live with them there. He wanted them to know His manifest presence in that place. It was meant to be heaven on earth, as the Lord Jesus taught his disciples to pray, "Your kingdom come, Your will be done on earth as it is in heaven" (Matt. 6:10). This theme can be traced throughout the Bible from beginning to end.

Where the presence of the Lord is, heaven is, because heaven is the dwelling place of God. Where God is, heaven is, and where heaven is, God is. The gospel of Matthew often refers to the kingdom of God interchangeably with the kingdom of heaven.

All of creation was meant for mankind in partnership with the Creator.

> *And God said, "See, I have given you*
> *every herb that yields seed which is on the face*
> *of all the earth, and every tree whose fruit*
> *yields seed; to you it shall be for food.*
> *Also, to every beast of the earth, to every bird*
> *of the air, and to everything that creeps*
> *on the earth, in which there is life, I have*
> *given every green herb for food," and it was so.*
> (Gen. 1:29–30).

Notice that the man was clearly able to hear the voice of the Lord, the One who created him. This is one of the benefits of His presence: to be able to hear His voice, to hear Him speaking to me. Jesus said in John 6:63, "The words that I speak to you are spirit, and they are life." Why was he able to say that? Because the words He spoke were the words of the spirit of God, Himself.

He says in John 12:49, "the Father who sent Me gave Me a command, what I should say and what I should speak." The Lord Jesus is not repeating Himself here. He is saying that not only does He say *what* his Father is saying but he says it *how* His Father is saying it. He doesn't put His own spin on it. He says it exactly how He hears it.

When He speaks, it is God speaking, just as it was God speaking to Adam at the beginning of creation. God spoke life into everything He made. Life that was meant to last forever—eternal life. Life that was never meant to be terminated by death.

God was providing all the food Adam and Eve would ever need forever. All the food every creature that had life in it would ever need forever. The man would not have to work for his food, nor hunt for it. There would be no hunting because there would be no killing—no humans killing animals for food and no animals killing other animals for food. God had created a quality of food in the herbs and the fruit of the trees that would provide a perfectly balanced source of healthy, life-sustaining nutrition for them.

This reminds us of the revelation the apostle John saw on the island of Patmos to which he was exiled for his witness of Christ.

> *And he showed me a pure river of water*
> *of life, clear as crystal, proceeding from*
> *the throne of God and of the Lamb.*
> *In the middle of its street [in the new Jerusalem*
> *on the new earth, under the new heavens],*
> *and on either side of the river, was the tree*
> *of life, which bore twelve fruits, each tree*
> *yielding its fruit every month. The leaves of*
> *the tree were for the healing of the nations.*
> (Rev. 22:1–2)

Here we see God, after a long detour, bringing us back to the beginning, providing us trees from which to eat, just as He did for Adam and Eve. And like Adam and Eve, all we will have to do is gather it, much like the children of Israel did in the wilderness when they gathered the manna that God rained down from heaven.

Mankind was to be God's partner in caring for and managing what God had created. All they had to do was work with it, and it would be blessed and flourish because God was in it.

In Genesis 1, God started with the heavens and the earth. He spoke light into existence where there was only darkness. This is one of the two primary characteristics of the nature of God: light and love. 1 John 1:5 says that "God is light and in Him is no darkness at *all*" (emphasis added). Not one shred of darkness. In fact, 1 Timothy 6:16 says that He dwells in "unapproachable light." It is so bright, so brilliant, that no one can stand in the full measure of the brightness of His presence.

What I find interesting to consider here is that when He said, "Let there be light," God was not talking about the daylight that is produced by the sun. Rather, He was talking about the light of His presence. It is the light of His presence that enlightens me from the darkness of ignorance and brings me to the knowledge of God.

Isaiah 9:2 says, "The people who walked in darkness have seen a great light; those who dwelt in the land of the shadow of death, upon them a light has shined." The people have seen a great light. I believe it is the light of His presence that is being spoken of here as well. Light is associated with life; darkness is associated with death. To be separated from the light of God's presence is death—spiritual death. Forever living in the torment and terror of darkness. That is hell—the absolute and total absence of light. The light of God's presence, His joy, His love, His peace. Forever living in the torment of darkness, fear, agony, and anxiety.

A further consideration for the possibility that God was not speaking of physical light when He said, "Let there be light," is in Genesis 1:2, where it says, "the Spirit of God was hovering over the face of the waters." When God shows up, there is light, the enlightenment, the awareness of His presence.

Genesis 1:16 says, "Then God made two great lights: the greater light [the sun] to rule the day, and the lesser light [the moon] to rule the night. He made the stars also." Genesis 1:17 goes on to say, "God set them in the firmament of the heavens to give light on the earth." Why would God need to do that if he created the sun in verse three of this chapter when He said, "Let there be light"? I believe that the sun and the moon and the stars were meant to bring light and life to the earth. His presence was meant to bring light and life to me forevermore. The first part of Psalm 27:1 says that the Lord is our light and our salvation. God's light brings salvation because we are enlightened by the truth that saves us from eternal death and brings us to eternal life.

The Lord Jesus, our Mediator, said in John 14:6, "I am the way, the truth, and the life. No one comes to the Father except through Me." Here we see, in Jesus, the supreme effort of God the Father to bring us back into His presence. To bring His presence back into us as revealed on the day of Pentecost spoken of in the book of Acts.

When the Day of Pentecost had fully come,
they were all with one accord in one place. And
suddenly there came a sound from heaven, as of a
rushing mighty wind, and it filled the whole house
where they were sitting. Then there appeared to
them divided tongues, as of fire, and one sat upon
each of them. And they were all filled with the
Holy Spirit and began to speak with other tongues,
as the Spirit gave them utterance.
(Act. 2:1-4)

It was a sound of heaven coming to earth, heaven coming back to earth after the Lord Jesus, our Mediator, had paid the price for our sin to free us from the penalty, which was death. And then He rose from the dead to break the power of sin over us, ascended back to heaven from whence He came, and sent the Holy Spirit to fill us with His presence.

So, going back to the beginning, God starts with light. The dark, empty, formless earth is now brought to life by the Light, and it is from there that all the rest of what He creates is brought to life, brought into existence. The light of His presence sparks the formation of the earth, day and night, seasons, seas, sea creatures, plants, animals, birds, all with reproductive power, and then finally man.

However, man was going to be made uniquely different, and distinct from everything else God had made. All that came before the making of man was made after its own kind.

But man was made after the God kind, a little lower than the angels, in the image and likeness of God. God was making children for Himself, for His glory and His pleasure, and for relationship with Him.

All of this was made for the man to enjoy and manage and have dominion over together with his wife, Eve, and the One who created it all. And it was God's original intent for it to be forever so.

Genesis 1:26 says, "Then God said, 'Let Us make man in Our image, according to Our likeness; let them have dominion over the fish of the sea, over the birds of the air, and over the cattle, over all the earth and over every creeping thing that creeps on the earth." How many believe God does what He says He will do? As it says in Isaiah 55:11, "So shall My word be that goes forth from My mouth; it shall not return to Me void, but it shall accomplish what I please, and it shall prosper in the thing for which I sent it." So, after God created everything else by His spoken word, He decided to make mankind, for whom all of this had been prepared so that we could have dominion over it.

And the LORD God formed man of the dust of the ground, and breathed into his nostrils the breath of life; and man became a living being. The LORD God planted a garden eastward in Eden, and there He put the man whom He had formed.
(Gen. 2:7–8)

God made the man to be an eternal being. When God breathed the breath of life into the man, He wasn't just breathing oxygen into his lungs, He was breathing His own eternal spirit into him, the Holy Spirit. This reminds us of what Jesus did after he rose from the dead. He appeared to His fearful disciples, as recorded in John's gospel chapter 20:21–22.

> *So Jesus said to them again, "Peace to you! As the Father has sent Me, I also send you." And when He had said this, He breathed on them, and said to them, "Receive the Holy Spirit."*

This was the same breath of the eternal God that breathed the breath of life into the first man, Adam.

Then God planted a garden for the man. The man didn't plant it, God planted it because that was to be the dwelling place of God with man. God put the man in the garden. The man didn't put himself there, God put him there to live with Him. This is where you're going to live, here in this garden with Me, in My presence. Can you imagine that? The manifest, continual, unbroken presence of God with him in the garden. A continual awareness of His presence with him. I am delighted with occasional manifestations of His presence in my life. I can only imagine the unspeakable joy of the constant, ongoing awareness of His presence. As Psalm 16:11 says, "In Your presence is *fullness* of joy" (emphasis added). Not just an occasional little bit, but a continual fullness of never-ending joy. All those who have died in Christ now enjoy this!

God brought the man into His heavenly presence, and this continues to be His desire. To bring us into His presence and His presence into us. To live in His presence, by His presence, and for His presence. This is the joy of the Lord, which is our strength. This is our continual pursuit, the pursuit of His presence in us and through us to others. It is out of God's presence that everything the man would ever need would be provided by the One who made him. The man was made to be totally dependent upon God, to be God's dependent just as children are the dependents of their parents.

Philippians 4:19 says, "And my God shall supply all your need according to His riches in glory by Christ Jesus."

Genesis 3:8 says that the man and woman "heard the sound of the LORD God walking in the garden." The word *sound* literally means *voice*.[1] They heard the voice of the Lord. They had the awesome privilege of hearing the voice of the Lord. It goes on to say, "in the cool of the day," which literally means as a breeze or wind blowing in the garden.[2] Again, we see this same wind of His presence blowing in the upper room in the second chapter of Acts, where Jesus's disciples were gathered together in one accord, with one purpose—to wait for the power of the Holy Spirit to descend upon them as Jesus had promised He would.

---

[1] Strong, James. "6963 קֹל (*kole*)," Strong's Hebrew: 6963. קֹל (*kole*) (Strong's Concordance, 2025), https://strongsconcordance.org/

[2] Strong, James. "7307 רוּחַ (*roo'-akh*)," Strong's Hebrew: 7307. רוּחַ (*roo'-akh*) (Strong's Concordance, 2025), https://strongsconcordance.org/

May I digress a bit here to talk about the power of the Holy Spirit? This is something that has been debated quite often among followers of Jesus. One argument states that we receive the Holy Spirit when we receive Jesus into our heart to be my Lord and Savior. As Jesus told Nicodemus in John 3, we are born again, born of the spirit, born from above. This is certainly true. However, I believe that this is speaking of the person of the Holy Spirit, who now lives in us and breathes in us eternal life.

I believe there is a difference between the person of the Holy Spirit and the power of the Holy Spirit. The Lord Jesus spoke of this in Acts 1:8 when He said, "You shall receive power when the Holy Spirit has come upon you." I believe there's a difference between the Holy Spirit being *in* me and *on* me. He is always in me, just as the Lord Jesus promised He would never leave me or forsake me. He would be with me always, even to the end of the world (Matt. 8:20). That is the ever-abiding presence of the Holy Spirit with me, helping me, comforting me, guiding me, teaching me, and bringing God's words to my remembrance.

However, in addition to His presence is the occasional manifestation and demonstration of the power of the Holy Spirit, as described in Acts 4:31, "And when they had prayed, the place where they were assembled together was shaken; and they were all filled with the Holy Spirit, and they spoke the word of God with boldness."

The word for boldness in Greek is *parrhesia* (par-rhay-see'-ah).[3] It means outspokenness, unreserved utterance, cheerful courage, and the absence of cowardice, timidity, or fear. These were followers of Christ. They already had the witness of the Holy Spirit living *in* them according to the gospel of John 20:22, where Jesus breathed on them and said, "Receive the Holy Spirit."

God then decided to make a helper for the man. "And the Lord God said, 'It is not good that man should be alone; I will make him a helper comparable to him'" (Gen. 2:18). I see an interesting parallel here where the wife that God is going to create for Adam is referred to as a "helper." The Lord Jesus uses a similar word in John 15:26. The word for helper in the Greek is *paraklétos* (par-ak'-lay-tos).[4] This word comes from *pará*, meaning "beside,"[5] and *kaléō*, which means "to call."[6] So, taken together, it means a calling to one's side, an intercessor, comforter, counselor.

God took one of Adam's ribs from his side and made it into a woman and brought her to the man to be by his side

---

[3] Strong, James. "3954 παῤῥησία (*par-rhay-see'-ah*)," Strong's Greek: 3954. παῤῥησία (*par-rhay-see'-ah*) (Strong's Concordance, 2025), https://strongsconcordance.org/

[4] Strong, James. "3875 παράκλητος (*par-ak'-lay-tos*)," Strong's Greek: 3875. παράκλητος (*par-ak'-lay-tos*) (Strong's Concordance, 2025), https://strongsconcordance.org/

[5] Strong, James. "3844 παρά (par-ah')," Strong's Greek: 3844. παρά (par-ah') (BibleHub, 2023), https://biblehub.com/greek/strongs/3844.htm.

[6] Strong, James. "2564 καλέω (kal-eh'-o)," Strong's Greek: 2564. καλέω (kal-eh'-o) (BibleHub, 2023), https://biblehub.com/greek/strongs/2564.htm.

to help him, comfort him and support him, much like the Holy Spirit does with us. Men tend to analyze things from a logical point of view. Women tend to analyze things from what feels right to them. They use intuition, thus providing another side to the decision-making process. This does not mean that men don't have feelings and women don't have logic. It simply means that men tend to lean more toward logic and women tend to lean more toward intuition. Several years ago, I decided, after some logical investigation, to invest in a small business venture. My wife did not have a good feeling about it and let me know it. I chose to ignore her advice and went ahead with it anyway. Well, I ended up wishing I had taken her advice, because it was a total bust. So, those of us who are husbands ought to be continually grateful for the wives that God has given us. As Proverbs 18:22 says, "He who finds a wife finds a good thing."

Once again, Adam didn't ask for a wife. God gave him one. Adam didn't even know what a woman was. Nor did he understand the concept of a wife in order to ask for one. All he knew was God, his Creator. This can serve as a good model for men today. Keep your eyes on God. Make Him and His will and His presence your primary pursuit and you won't have to look for a wife. God has already found one for you, and when the time comes, He will bring her to you. (Gen. 2:22)

Proverbs 31:10 speaks to this issue as well. Who can find a virtuous wife, a wife of noble character? A wife of valor in the sense of all forms of excellence. Who can find such a wife for you men? God can!

And Adam said:
"This is now bone of my bones
And flesh of my flesh;
She shall be called Woman,
Because she was taken out of Man."
Therefore a man shall leave his father and mother
and be joined to his wife, and they shall become
one flesh. (Genesis 2:23–24)

Bone of my bone, flesh of my flesh, partners in life, walking together. As Amos 3:3 says, "Can two walk together, unless they are agreed?"

As quoted above, Genesis 2:24 says that the man shall be joined to his wife. That word *joined* is a strong word. It means to keep close, stick to, stay in close contact, communication, to stick with like super glue.[7] What is joined together is not meant to be separated. It is meant to be permanently bonded together.

When God brought to Adam the woman he had taken out of him, they were not meant to be separated, just as two items superglued together are not meant to be separated. If we wanted to separate them, we would not glue them together.

---

[7] Jack W. Hayford et al., *New Spirit-Filled Life Bible: New International Version* (Nashville: Thomas Nelson, 2015).

The Lord Jesus reiterates this same theme in Matthew 19:5–6, and He adds, "What God has joined together, let not man separate." Several Sources indicate that 40-45 percent of all first marriages in the United States end in divorce. Additionally, second marriages end in divorce at an even higher rate of 60 to 70 percent.

If we separate what God has joined together, much harm can come as a result. Unfortunately, not only can much harm come to the man and woman who separate, but collateral damage can come to the children of divorce.

Studies show that children whose parents divorce are, on average, at higher risk for a range of difficulties compared to peers from continuously married families. They are:

- more likely to experience behavioral and physical complaints, such as insomnia, chronic stomach aches, and headaches
- more likely to have lower academic achievements and are twice as likely to drop out of high school
- are at increased risk of smoking, drinking, and drug abuse during adolescence
- are at an elevated risk of attempting suicide
- more likely to have trouble fitting into peer groups
- more likely to experience mental health problems, anxiety, and depression as teens
- more likely to end up in prison

What God has joined together, let not man separate!!

Are there times when divorce is necessary? Certainly, there are. There may be extenuating circumstances, such as mental and physical abuse, addictions, or other threatening behaviors. Still, let couples make every attempt at restoration and revitalization, so that the exceptions may be few and far between.

The oneness of marriage was to reflect our oneness with God, our marriage to Him, which is going to be greatly celebrated at the Marriage Supper of the Lamb in heaven (Rev. 19:9). And then we see in Revelation 21:1–2 that the apostle John sees a new heaven and a new earth, and the holy city, the new Jerusalem, coming down out of heaven prepared as a bride adorned for her Husband.

Agreement is the key to oneness, to becoming one with another. Agreement starts with both the man and the woman being in agreement with God, one with Him in will and purpose. His will is my will; His way is my way; His word is my word. We agree that in all things we will seek the will, the way, and the word of God.

God intended us to live in agreement with Him. When God told Adam and Eve they could eat from any tree in the garden except from the Tree of the Knowledge of Good and Evil, His expectation was that they would agree. God had done his part. He created and provided every tree they would ever need for all eternity. His expectation was that they would do their part. They would stay in alignment with Him, in submission to Him. This is the key to living in His presence. The presence of the Lord is much more than a feeling; it is a condition, and that condition is being in His will. We stay in agreement with Him and refuse to go outside the boundary of His will.

> *Now the word of the LORD came to Jonah the son of Amittai, saying, "Arise, go to Nineveh, that great city, and cry out against it; for their wickedness has come up before Me." But Jonah arose to flee to Tarshish from the presence of the LORD. He went down to Joppa, and found a ship going to Tarshish; so he paid the fare, and went down into it, to go with them to Tarshish from the presence of the LORD.*
> (Jona. 1:1–3)

Notice that it says that Jonah did not do what God told him to do, but he fled to Tarshish **from the presence of the Lord**. There is a direct connection between the presence of the Lord and the boundary of His will. When I choose to go outside the boundary of His will, I am leaving His presence. His presence is no longer with me. I no longer have the benefit of His presence. I no longer have the benefit of His help. I no longer have the benefit of His protection. I am on my own, and I am now an open target for trouble. Not only trouble for myself, but trouble for the people around me—my wife, my children, whoever is associated with me. We see this as Jonah's story continues,

But the Lord sent out a great wind on the sea,
and there was a mighty tempest on the sea,
so that the ship was about to be broken up.
Then the mariners were afraid; and every man
cried out to his god, and threw the cargo
that was in the ship into the sea, to lighten
the load. But Jonah had gone down into the lowest
parts of the ship, had lain down, and was fast
asleep. So the captain came to him, and said to
him, "What do you mean, sleeper? Arise, call on
your God; perhaps your God will consider us,
so that we may not perish." And they said to one
another, "Come, let us cast lots, that we may know
for whose cause this trouble has come upon us."
So they cast lots, and the lot fell on Jonah.
(Jona. 1:4–7)

I become a troublemaker for those around me when I am outside the boundary of the will of God, and ultimately people will have to disassociate with me. When the mariners cast Jonah into the sea, "the sea ceased from its raging" (Jonah 1:15). When I am willing to stay in agreement with the will of God and obey His commands and His word, I will have the benefit of the joy, peace, and love I find in His presence. This is God's intended norm for His children—righteousness, peace, and joy in the Holy Spirit (Rom.14:17).

This is His way for us in marriage as well. A wife may not agree with her husband in certain matters, and it is important for her to express that to him. However, if he does not change his mind, because she is an agreement with God to honor her husband as she would the Lord, she submits to him. The agreement they made in their marriage covenant will remain intact. The wife can rest confidently in the fact that her willingness to honor God by honoring her husband will put her in a great state of favor with God. And if her husband is walking and living in agreement with God, he will love his wife as Christ loves His bride and be willing to humbly lay down his pride if she was right in a matter.

As I mentioned previously, such was the case several years ago when I had the opportunity for what I thought would be a profitable business venture. My wife didn't share that same sentiment and let me know, not in a belligerent or dishonoring way, but respectfully disagreed and didn't think we should do it. However, I persistently insisted that it was the right move to make and went ahead with it. My wife simply said, "OK." No argument, no fuss, no muss. Well, it only took about three months for that venture to go belly up. However, the beauty of it was that my wife didn't hit me with the "I told you so" line which she would've been perfectly justified to do. She simply said, "I'm sorry that happened." So was I. However, I was more sorry that I hadn't listened to her, and I let her know that.

God made Adam to love his wife. And God made Eve to respect and honor her husband. What a husband needs most from his wife is respect, and what a wife needs most from her husband is love (Eph. 5:22–25).

A husband continues to love his wife, even when she may not be so lovable because he loves God and loves God's command to love his wife. A wife continues to respect her husband, even when he is not so deserving of that respect, because she loves God, and loves God's command to respect her husband.

This is also God's way for us to relate to one another as the church of the Lord Jesus Christ. We have grievously witnessed too many church "splits" or "divorces" over disagreements. We may not always agree about the issues, but we can and must be "endeavoring to keep the unity of the Spirit in the bond of peace" (Eph. 4:3). That word *endeavor* means to make every effort, to strain every nerve to maintain the unity of the spirit in the bond of peace.[8]

Psalm 133:1 says, "Behold how good and how pleasant it is for brethren [generic term for men and women] to dwell together in unity!" Verse three of that same psalm says, "For there the LORD commanded the blessing."

Sadly, Adam and Eve were deceived into breaking their unity with the One who created them by disobeying His command to not eat from the Tree of the Knowledge of Good and Evil, and so came the separation.

---

[8] Jack W. Hayford et al., *New Spirit-Filled Life Bible: New International Version* (Nashville: Thomas Nelson, 2015).

Chapter Two

The Separation

*I*t was never God's intent for heaven to be separated from earth, for mankind to be separated from God, or for us to be separated from one another by death. We were meant to live with God in His manifest presence forever. We were meant to live with one another forever. Our eternal existence was meant to be characterized by heaven on earth, enjoying all the benefits of heaven.

As mentioned above, Psalm 16:11 says that in the presence of the Lord, there is fullness of joy. There is no sadness or sorrow in heaven because there is no reason for it. There is no fear or worry or anxiety in heaven because heaven is permeated with the warmth of the perfect love of God. There are no hospitals, prisons, police stations, doctors, or funeral homes in heaven, because there is no sickness, disease, or death in heaven.

A predominant theme of the Bible is bringing heaven back to earth, mankind back to God, and us back to one another. It is how the Bible starts out in Genesis and how it ends up in

Revelation with a long detour in between. Furthermore, His ultimate plan of restoration will be mediated by one Man, the Man Christ Jesus, the Mediator. He was the only one qualified to mediate the restoration because the restoration would require one who knew no sin, another sinless Adam, a last Adam to pay the penalty of death incurred by the first Adam's disobedience to the command of God. God so loved the people of the world that he was willing to give his only begotten sinless Son to us to release us from the penalty of eternal death, which is eternal separation from God with no recourse. The obedient for the disobedient, the deserving for the undeserving, the worthy for the unworthy, the hope for the hopeless, the help for the helpless.

> *In this manner, therefore, pray:*
> *Our Father in heaven,*
> *Hallowed be Your name.*
> *Your kingdom come.*
> *Your will be done*
> *On earth as it is in heaven.*
> (Matthe. 6:9–10)

Here we see the Lord Jesus setting the priority in prayer, acknowledging God as our Father, our Creator, the Holy One. And then praying for His kingdom and will to be done on earth as it is in heaven. Bringing heaven back to earth, not so much as a place, but as a people within whom His heavenly kingdom could be expressed, just as it was in Him, the Man from heaven.

Heaven's Separation from Earth

> *Then the LORD God took the man and put him*
> *in the garden of Eden to tend and keep it.*
> *And the LORD God commanded the man,*
> *saying, "Of every tree of the garden you may*
> *freely eat; but of the tree of the knowledge*
> *of good and evil you shall not eat, for in the day*
> *that you eat of it you shall surely die."*
> (Gen. 2:15–17)

God has created a garden for the man and put the man in that garden with Him where He's provided everything the man would ever need. The man didn't have to plant anything. God planted it, and made it grow. However, here we see for the first time God giving the man a command: "You shall NOT eat." Prior to this, God had said, "You may freely eat." So God is establishing an order, a chain of command—His authority over the man. "I am God, and you are My Man, under My authority. I made you to be dependent upon Me for all that you need. I didn't make you to be independent of Me. You can't handle that; it's too much for you." Just as children are dependent on their parents, so we are dependent upon God. Again, as the Lord Jesus taught us to pray, "Give us this day [today], our *daily* bread" (Matt. 6:11, emphasis added).

God made the garden for the man out of his great love for him. He knew what was good for the man and what was bad for the man, and it was his expectation that the man would believe him and trust him just as parents can have that same expectation for their children. In Jeremiah 29:11 God says, "I know the plans I have for you…plans to prosper you and not to harm you" (NIV). God will not steer us wrong. He knows exactly what He's doing and exactly what we need, even if we have no idea what He's doing, and it is totally contrary to what we think He should do. In Isaiah 55:8 God says, "My thoughts are not your thoughts, nor are your ways My ways." And He goes on to tell us in verse nine that His ways are higher than ours and His thoughts are higher than our thoughts. My ways and thoughts have only a short-term effect in mind. God's ways and thoughts affect eternity. It is the devil who seeks to entice us to trust in our own ways and thoughts, just as he did in the garden, leading to his demise and ours. As Proverbs 14:12 tells us, "There is a way that seems right to a man, but its end is the way of death."

> *"How you are fallen from heaven,*
> *O Lucifer, son of the morning!*
> *How you are cut down to the ground,*
> *You who weakened the nations!*
> *For you have said in your heart:*
> *'I will ascend into heaven,*
> *I will exalt my throne above the stars of God;*
> *I will also sit on the mount of the congregation*
> *On the farthest sides of the north;*
> *I will ascend above the heights of the clouds,*
> *I will be like the Most High.'" (Isaia. 14:12–14)*

Lucifer was cast out of heaven to the ground and into the darkest depths of the earth, suggesting that he was there before God brought form and order and light to the earth. No wonder John Milton, in his poem "Paradise Lost," refers to Satan as the Prince of Darkness.

Ezekiel brings the following word of the Lord to the king of Tyre:

> *"You were the seal of perfection,*
> *Full of wisdom and perfect in beauty.*
> *You were in Eden, the garden of God;*
> *Every precious stone was your covering:*
> *The sardius, topaz, and diamond,*
> *Beryl, onyx, and jasper,*
> *Sapphire, turquoise, and emerald with gold.*
> *The workmanship of your timbrels and pipes*
> *Was prepared for you on the day you were created.*
> *"You were the anointed cherub who covers;*
> *I established you;*
> *You were on the holy mountain of God;*
> *You walked back and forth in the midst of fiery stones.*
> *You were perfect in your ways from the day you were created,*
> *Till iniquity was found in you."*
> (Ez. 28:12-15)

A few verses later, the same word continues, "Your heart was lifted up because of your beauty; you corrupted your wisdom for the sake of your splendor; I cast you to the ground, I laid you before kings, that they might gaze at you" (Ez. 28:17). This portion of scripture is speaking of the king of Tyre in the natural realm, but I believe in the spiritual realm it is referring to Satan's fall from heaven. He was lifted up with pride, thinking he could dethrone God and take his place. This is the origin of the spirit of Antichrist that will be in the world at the end of the ages. One who will be lifted up with pride, thinking he could dethrone Christ and take his place.

Proverbs 16:18 says, "Pride goes before destruction." If we don't kill pride in our lives, it will end up killing us—killing our connection with God, our Savior. James 4:6 says, "God resists the proud, but gives grace to the humble."

When Ezekiel says that Lucifer was in Eden, this is a reference to the presence of God he enjoyed before his rebellion and banishment to the earth. So, when God planted the garden of Eden upon the earth to live with Adam and his wife, it seems to me that the serpent was already on the earth to which he had been cast from heaven. God allowed him to be there. God allowed him to slither into the garden to tempt Eve and her husband to eat from the tree from which He had commanded them not to eat. Why would God allow that, and take the chance of spoiling everything? I believe it was because it was God's intention to test them and prove their love for Him freely without any coercion on His part. Unfortunately for them, and for all of us, they failed that test. Thank God that He had another Adam, the last Adam, the Mediator, who would come into the world and not fail, making it possible for us to be restored to right relationship with God.

We see the effects of the Fall in our world today in an almost unprecedented way. I don't know if we have ever seen such rebellion against God's law—and the law in general—as we do today. And all this is due to one man's and one woman's decision, bringing sin, rebellion, and death into the world. 1 John 3:4 says, in part, "sin is lawlessness." Lawlessness is a refusal to be ruled and to be under authority. James 1:15 says that "sin, when it is full-grown, brings forth death." Death is eternal separation from God.

God warned the man, and the man informed his wife that they were not to eat from the Tree of the Knowledge of Good and Evil. It was the one tree, as appealing as it was, that had the potential to separate mankind from God, heaven from earth, and mankind from one another.

That is why God sternly warned them not to eat from that tree. "For in the day you eat from it you shall surely die" (Gen. 2:17). A more accurate interpretation from the original language is "dying you shall die."[9] In other words, "you will be dying while you live until you finally die." From the moment I am born, I am dying. My life and everything I do and anything I accomplish will ultimately be futile because I only have death to look forward to. This all came from Adam being cut off and cast out of the presence of the Lord, who was the source of life.

Once again, why would God allow this? I believe it is because they were created in His image and likeness, which

---

[9] Jack W. Hayford et al., *New Spirit-Filled Life Bible: New International Version* (Nashville: Thomas Nelson, 2015).

included the power to choose. They were not programmed robots. They were not beasts like the rest of life upon the earth. He made them distinct from beasts by giving them the power of words and a will. It was God's desire that they would believe Him and love Him enough to obey Him. They had to make that choice. They had to be put to the test. It could not be by coercion or convenience; it had to be by concession. They had to concede to the will and command of God no matter how good that tree looked. Their faith in, love for, and obedience to God's command had to be the higher priority, but they failed. The Tempter's plan succeeded. And so now a Mediator would be required to reverse that one decision that led to eternal separation from God.

Then to Adam He said, "Because you have heeded the voice of your wife, and have eaten from the tree of which I commanded you, saying, 'You shall not eat of it':
"Cursed is the ground for your sake;
In toil you shall eat of it
All the days of your life.
Both thorns and thistles it shall bring forth for you,
And you shall eat the herb of the field."
(Genesi. 3:17–18)

Oh, how crucial it is whose voice we are listening to. How crucial it is who has influence in our lives. Eve had already eaten from the tree. Her husband now had a choice to make. Was he going to listen to his wife or to God? Did his wife persuade him as the serpent had persuaded her?

Did Adam consult with the One who created him to know whether He had changed His mind, and it was now OK to eat from it? Why did Adam choose to listen to his wife?

Genesis 2:23 says that when God brought Eve to Adam, he described her as bone of his bones and flesh of his flesh, which suggests that it would possibly have been quite painful to be separated from her. It is natural to want to avoid pain. Adam may very well have chosen to avoid the pain of being separated from Eve over obeying the command of God. However, I don't know whether Adam considered or knew that his separation from Eve would be temporary, but his separation from God would be forever. We live and die by the choices we make!

The tragic result of Adam's decision to listen to the voice of his wife is that now the ground is cursed because the favor and presence of the Lord has withdrawn from it. It has now fallen into the domain of the "Prince of the Power of the Air." God had given Adam and Eve dominion over the earth and everything on it. Satan's plan all along was to steal their dominion. In John 10:10, the Lord Jesus says that the thief (Satan) comes only to steal, kill, and destroy. That is his only agenda.

Heaven is now separated from earth, and the ground is cursed and no longer under the blessing of God, and therefore, no longer a blessing to the man. He would now have to work the ground for his food, and the ground is not going to be so cooperative. There are going to be thorns, thistles, and weeds—unwanted, uncontrollable invaders in his effort to grow food. There are going to be droughts, floods, hurricanes, tornadoes, and earthquakes, none of which God originally intended.

> *The earth also was corrupt before God, and the*
> *earth was filled with violence. So God looked upon*
> *the earth, and indeed it was corrupt; for all flesh*
> *had corrupted their way on the earth.*
> (Genesi. 6:11–12)

The earth was corrupt. In the Hebrew, that means it was ruined, decaying, rotting, spoiled.[10] All because heaven was now separated from the earth by one decision.

1 Samuel 15:23 says that "rebellion is as the sin of witchcraft." Rebellion is the desire to have control and to be in control. It is a refusal to be in subjection or submission to authority, but rather, an act that takes the authority. In essence, it is the attitude and disposition that says, "No one is going to tell me what to do." Rebellion will always cause heaven to withdraw.

God never intended for us to know trouble and tragedy and heartbreak. In fact, it broke His heart when the man and woman He created to be his very own children chose to disobey Him and come under the dominion of the evil one, much like parents can grieve over their children's choices that bring hurt and heartbreak. Heaven has withdrawn from

---

[10] Strong, James. "7843 שָׁחַת (*shaw-khath'*)," Strong's Hebrew: 7843. שָׁחַת (*shaw-khath'*) (Strong's Concordance, 2025), https://strongsconcordance.org/

the earth, and now the principle of death would spoil and corrupt everything God had created. What God intended to last forever would die. It would be doomed to destruction along with the heavens above it.

The Lord Jesus said in Matthew 24:35, "Heaven and earth will pass away…" He repeats this in Mark 13:31 and Luke 21:33. 1 John 2:17 says, "the world is passing away." Perhaps one of the strongest words in this regard is 2 Peter 3:10–12:

But the day of the Lord will come as a thief in the night, in which the heavens will pass away with a great noise, and the elements will melt with fervent heat; both the earth and the works that are in it will be burned up.

Therefore, since all these things will be dissolved, what manner of persons ought you to be in holy conduct and godliness, looking for and hastening the coming of the day of God, because of which the heavens will be dissolved, being on fire, and the elements will melt with fervent heat?

1 Corinthians 7:31 says that "the form of this world is passing away." It is deteriorating much like things in our home deteriorate. Nothing in this world lasts forever because heaven has been separated from earth. A hallmark of heaven is its eternal quality. Therefore, whatever is separated from heaven passes away. God made everything to last forever. He never meant for anyone or anything to die.

> *So God created man in His own image; in the*
> *image of God He created him; male and female*
> *He created them. Then God blessed them, and*
> *God said to them, "Be fruitful and multiply; fill*
> *the earth and subdue it; have dominion over the*
> *fish of the sea, over the birds of the air, and over*
> *every living thing that moves on the earth. "*
> (Genesi. 1:27–28)

God made the man and then made the woman out of the man. In this day and age, we have forgotten the One who made us because we have rejected the One who made us. We act as if we are self-made, and it all stems from the first man and woman's decision to reject the command of God to not eat from the Tree of the Knowledge of Good and Evil. Knowledge became their God, based on human reason, logic, and what they knew through their senses.

When heaven is removed from earth, there is no knowledge of God, no influence for faith in God. The earth is returning to the chaos and disorder out of which God brought it. God made the man and the woman to subdue the earth and have dominion over everything that moves upon it, including the serpent, the devil. If they had listened to the command of God, the devil would have never become the Prince of the Power of the Air over the earth. He would have never had that influence, that dominion. I believe that eventually God would have disposed of him, just as he will dispose of him in the lake of fire, but without having caused all of the grief, destruction, and death this world has known up to this time.

However, because the first man and woman succumbed to the trickery of the serpent, they unwittingly surrendered the God-given dominion they had over the earth and all life upon the earth. He is now the Prince of the Power of the Air, and he now has dominion over the earth and all life upon the earth, including the man and the woman, and all succeeding generations to follow. The authority of heaven has been separated from the earth to the grief of all heaven.

We might ask, "Why is heaven grieved; why is God grieved? God knows the beginning from the end. He is the beginning and the end. The Lamb was slain before the foundation of the world. He is going to turn it around." All of this is true. However, God is grieved over sin because mankind is going to suffer. There's going to be pain. There is going to be heartache, sickness, disease, and death. Mankind could've been spared all of this if Adam and Eve had just listened to God.

We see this in the Gospel of John, chapter 11, with the story of Lazarus, who died from a sickness before the Lord Jesus arrived on the scene. Martha and Mary were beside themselves with grief, saying to Jesus, "Lord, if you had just been here, our brother would not have died." Jesus knew he was going to raise Lazarus from the dead, and yet, verse 35, the shortest verse in the Bible, says "Jesus wept." Why was He weeping? I don't usually picture Jesus crying, and yet, here He is, weeping, fully identifying with their grief. The apostle Paul says in Romans 12:15 that we should "weep with those who weep," which I believe is exactly what the Lord Jesus is doing here, weeping with his grieving friends. Hebrews 4:15 says, "For we do not have a High Priest who cannot sympathize with our weaknesses." God is not a cold, unfeeling God. After all, we have been made in His likeness and image, and we have feelings. It follows that He also experiences emotions.

> *Then the LORD saw that the wickedness of man*
> *was great in the earth, and that every intent of the*
> *thoughts of his heart was only evil continually.*
> *And the LORD was sorry that He had made man on*
> *the earth, and He was grieved in His heart.*
> (Genesi. 6:5–6)

God was grieved in his heart. The original Hebrew suggests that God had continual pain in His heart.[11] His heart was broken, much like a parent's heart is broken over a wayward child.

Man's Separation from God

Genesis 2:15 says, "Then the LORD God took the man and put him in the garden of Eden to tend and keep it." As we mentioned previously, man was created to be God's companion and partner in caring for what God had created. Genesis 2:19 says, "Out of the ground the LORD God formed every beast of

---

[11] Jack W. Hayford et al., *New Spirit-Filled Life Bible: New International Version* (Nashville: Thomas Nelson, 2015).

the field and every bird of the air, and brought them to Adam to see what he would call them. And whatever Adam called each living creature, *that was its name*" (emphasis added).

Adam had the full support and authority of the One who created him, because he was fully in step with and in right relationship with Him. There was not yet any sin factor to separate him from the mind and will of God.

This reminds us of 1 Corinthians 15:45, where it refers to Jesus as the last Adam, who would not fail to obey God as the first Adam did. So, there would never be the need for another Adam. The last Adam, this sinless Son of God, Jesus, would not fall prey to the tempter in the wilderness. He would fully obey the will of the One who sent Him into the world. John 12:49 says, "I have not spoken on My own authority; but the Father who sent Me gave Me a command, what I should say and what I should speak." Whatever Jesus said came to pass, because He only said what He heard his Father saying, and what the Father says, goes! God said, "Let there be light," and there was light. In fact, everything God created was created by what He said, by His word.

> *Now when Jesus had entered Capernaum, a*
> *centurion came to Him, pleading with Him,*
> *saying, "Lord, my servant is lying at home*
> *paralyzed, dreadfully tormented."*
>
> *And Jesus said to him, "I will come and heal him."*

The centurion answered and said, "Lord, I am not
worthy that You should come under my roof. But
only speak a word, and my servant will be healed.
For I also am a man under authority, having
soldiers under me. And I say to this one, 'Go,' and
he goes; and to another, 'Come,' and he comes;
and to my servant, 'Do this,' and he does it."
(Matt. 8:5–10)

This is the restoration of the authority the first Adam had in the garden of the presence of God. Whatever Adam called each creature, that was its name!

The first Adam had God-given authority that was meant for all his successors to possess. But sin came in and separated him from God and his God-given authority.

Genesis 1:26 says, "Let Us make man in Our image, according to Our likeness." God decided to have children whom He would love. He expected that they, in turn, would love Him, just as parents have children and love them with the expectation that their love will be reciprocated by their children.

God made Adam and Eve to bear his likeness, to look like Him, not in a physical sense, but in a behavioral sense— to be like Him. The Lord Jesus said in John 14:9, "He who has seen Me has seen the Father." He was not talking about His physical appearance. He was talking about hearing the words that He spoke and the works that He did. Mark 6:2 says, "When the Sabbath had come, He began to teach in the synagogue. And many hearing Him were astonished, saying, 'Where did this Man get these things? And what wisdom is this which is given to Him, that such mighty works are performed by His hands!'" It was in this sense that Jesus was bearing the likeness of His Father. It is much the same with children who bear the likeness of their parents, not just in a physical sense, but in their similar character traits, good or bad. It is hard to deny our genetic makeup, genealogy, and environmental influences. They all play a part in shaping us.

If you look at the genealogy of the Man, Christ Jesus, listed in Luke chapter 3, it begins by listing Him (supposedly) as the son of Joseph, who was the son of Heli, and so on down the line until we come to the son of Seth. The son of Seth, who was the son of Adam who was the son of God. God had a son, he enjoined a wife to him and from them, He intended to have a multitude of children (Genesis 1:28). He wanted Adam to fill the earth with His children from his loins.

His children would rule His earth because they would have His authority, His wisdom, and His knowledge by virtue of their connection and communion with Him. How else would Adam know what to name every creature upon the earth? He received knowledge from God because he was in direct communication with God.

This was the eternal plan of God: to have His children live together with Him, through Him, by Him, and for Him forever. However, God would not force them to do so any more than good parents would force or manipulate their children to do so. They would have to do it willingly, because in creating the man and the woman in His own likeness, it meant they had the ability to say no to God, and that would be put to the test in the Garden.

> *And the* Lord *God commanded the man, saying,*
> *"Of every tree of the garden you may freely eat;*
> *but of the tree of the knowledge of good and*
> *evil you shall not eat, for in the day that you eat*
> *of it you shall surely die."*
> (Gen. 2:16–17)

We see here, as we have said previously, that God was giving them a command for two reasons. The first reason was to warn them of the consequences of eating from the Tree of the Knowledge of Good and Evil. "Dying you shall surely die." We might be tempted to ask the question, "Why did God plant the Tree of the Knowledge of Good and Evil?" Not only that, but right in the middle of the garden next to the Tree of Life?

Let's look at Deuteronomy 30:19, which says, "I call heaven and earth as witnesses today against you, that I have set before you life and death, blessing and cursing; therefore choose life, that both you and your descendants may live." God knew something Adam and Eve didn't. There was a snake in the grass in this garden, and it was going to tempt them to eat from that tree. Had Lucifer not rebelled against God in heaven, there would be no need for the Tree of the Knowledge of Good and Evil because there would be no evil. But Lucifer did rebel. God knew this, but Adam and Eve didn't. They had to trust the God who created them without knowing why. After all, isn't that what real trust is—trusting the character and nature of the One who commands us, without having to know why? Eventually, we will find out why without the regret of having found out for ourselves as Adam and Eve did. In their case, the regret was eternal.

God knows more than we do. That's why He's God, and we're not. There are things that look good to us, seem right to us, that are wrong. Proverbs 14:12 says, "There is a way that seems right to a man, but its end is the way of death." We cannot trust our human reasoning and natural senses when it comes to spiritual matters concerning God's will and desires for us. What I want is not what He wants. My way is not His way. The way I think is not the way He thinks. The only way His way becomes my way, and His thoughts become my thoughts, and His desires become my desires is through the method the apostle Paul declares in Galatians: "I have been crucified with Christ; it is no longer I who live, but Christ lives in me; and the life which I now live in the flesh I live by faith in the Son of God, who loved me and gave Himself for me" (2:20). Adam and Eve were going to be faced with a choice—would they listen to God or would they listen to the Tempter?

The second reason for God's command was to show whether they loved Him more than what He was withholding from them. Did they love Him for who He was to them, their Creator Father, or just for what He could do for them? We should not be surprised if God withholds or denies something we've asked of Him from time to time. God is very possibly testing us to prove that we love Him for Him and Him alone.

Job experienced this when Satan came before the throne of God and accused him of being devoted to God because of what God had done for him and not out of a pure heart. Satan is quoted as saying, "Take it all away from him (Job) and he will curse you to your face" (Job 1:11). Satan is suggesting that Job doesn't really love God for who he is, but only for what he provides.

Now the serpent was more cunning than any beast of the field which the Lord God had made. And he said to the woman, "Has God indeed said, 'You shall not eat of every tree of the garden'?"

And the woman said to the serpent, "We may eat the fruit of the trees of the garden; but of the fruit of the tree which is in the midst of the garden, God has said, 'You shall not eat it, nor shall you touch it, lest you die.'"

Then the serpent said to the woman, "You will not surely die. For God knows that in the day you eat of it your eyes will be opened, and you will be like God, knowing good and evil."

So when the woman saw that the tree was good
for food, that it was pleasant to the eyes, and a
tree desirable to make one wise, she took of its
fruit and ate. She also gave to her husband with
her, and he ate. Then the eyes of both of them
were opened, and they knew that they were naked;
and they sewed fig leaves together and made
themselves coverings.
(Gen. 3:1–7)

Here we see that the serpent deceived Eve into thinking that God was withholding something good from her— good for food, good to look at, good for knowledge. Not everything that looks good ends up being good.

Do not love the world or the things in
the world. If anyone loves the world,
the love of the Father is not in him. For all
that is in the world—the lust of the flesh,
the lust of the eyes, and the pride of life—
is not of the Father but is of the world.
(1 John 2:15–16)

Once again, I have a choice to make. Am I going to love the world and the things of the world? Am I going to live my life for riches, pleasure, and luxury, or am I going to love God, and prove it by living my life for Him?

Eve ate of the forbidden fruit of the Tree of the Knowledge of Good and Evil, and gave it to her husband, and he ate it.

When they ate from the tree, their eyes were opened, and they knew they were naked. They knew they had made the wrong choice. They were exposed. They felt the shame of that exposure, and they hid from the presence of the Lord. The separation of man from God had begun.

The Lord God sought them out to call them to account. Genesis 3:9 says that the Lord called to Adam and said to him, "Where are you?" It wasn't so much that God was asking him his location, but the position of his heart and who he had been listening to.

> *And He said, "Who told you that you were naked? Have you eaten from the tree of which I commanded you that you should not eat?"*
>
> *Then the man said, "The woman whom You gave to be with me, she gave me of the tree, and I ate."*
> (Gen. 3:11-12)

The man pointed to the woman, the woman pointed to the serpent, and God judged them all. We can't blame someone else for what we have done. We have to take responsibility for our own actions; that's what confession is. 1 John 1:9 says, "If we confess our sins, He is faithful and just to forgive us our sins and to cleanse us from all unrighteousness."

It is crucial that we be careful to whom we listen. We must only listen to those voices that are in agreement with the voice of the Lord, which we hear in our heart and read in His word. No matter how good or how appealing a voice may sound, we must block it out if it does not line up with God's voice.

So God pronounced judgment upon the man, the woman, and the serpent. However, the final judgment was the worst of all.

> *Then the LORD God said, "Behold, the man*
> *has become like one of Us, to know good and evil.*
> *And now, lest he put out his hand and take*
> *also of the tree of life, and eat, and live forever"*
> *—therefore the LORD God sent him out of the*
> *garden of Eden to till the ground from*
> *which he was taken. So He drove out the man;*
> *and He placed cherubim at the east of the garden*
> *of Eden, and a flaming sword which turned*
> *every way, to guard the way to the tree of life.*
> (Genesi. 3:22–24)

The man has now become like one of Us. He now knows what We know, but it has spoiled him and everything that We created for him. It has ruined him and overtaken him because it was not meant for him.

There are some things that are not meant for us. There are some things that are meant for us, but we're not ready for them. They would ruin us. Joseph wasn't ready for the fulfillment of the dreams of greatness when he had those dreams as a teenager. There had to be a time of preparation so that it wouldn't go to his head and cause him to fall.

Joseph never forgot his days in the pit and the prison, and that's what kept him in the palace.

The Lord Jesus made a similar statement in John 16:12, "I still have many things to say to you, but you cannot bear them now." He was saying, in essence, "You're not ready for them now." There are some things that God knows we're not ready for and that's why He withholds them from us. We might think we can handle them, but God knows better. He knows us better than we know ourselves. He knows our hearts and understands the intent of our thoughts, as it says in 1 Chronicles 28:9. In other words, He not only knows what we think, He knows why we think what we think. He knows there are some thoughts that would ruin us and ultimately separate us from Him if He granted the fulfillment of them.

And that is exactly what happened with Adam. God had to drive him out of the garden of His presence. Adam made his choice and there was no turning back. God had warned him that he would die the death of separation from His presence forever if he chose to disobey His command. It was a fatal decision, and God had to be true to His word.

Adam and his wife were now on their own, no longer knowing the benefit of the presence of the Lord, and it wasn't going to be easy for them. No longer knowing the fullness of joy found in His presence. No longer knowing the warmth and comfort of His presence. No longer knowing the peace of His presence. They were now sad and cold, naked and afraid, worried and anxious—none of which God had ever intended for them to experience. That is why He said to them to stay away from that Tree of Knowledge. It's not always good to know everything. There are some things I wish I never knew.

Once sin entered the world, Adam had to provide for himself and his wife, and it wouldn't going to be easy. Now his wife would have pain in childbirth. There would be stress and strain and suffering and the sting of death—all because they had made one choice to know good **and** evil. The evil spoiled the good. As the apostle Paul declares in Romans 7:21, "Although I want to do good, evil is right there with me" (NIV).

In spite of all of this, God was merciful to the man and woman and, subsequently, to the rest of humanity, by keeping them from eating from the Tree of Life. This would have kept them forever in a state of damnation, with no hope of restoration. God had a Mediator, a Lamb prepared for sacrifice **before** the foundation of the world, before any of this ever took place. He knew that the man and woman He had created were going to fail to obey His command.

Genesis 6:5 says, "Then the Lord saw that the wickedness of man was great in the earth, and that every intent of the thoughts of his heart was only evil continually." Here we see the awful effects of man's separation from God—a progressive degeneration of the human race. We see that degeneration proceeding rapidly in our society today. Mankind and government actively marginalize and separate God from society. We hear the term "separation of church and state," which was originally meant to keep the government from interfering with or having influence over the church. It was not meant, as it is often used today, to keep the church from having any influence upon the governing powers of our nation. Our nation was founded upon Judeo-Christian principles and values to guide our governance. Sadly, at this point, we have pretty much abandoned the guidance of Judeo-Christian values in our governance, and this has led to more and more corruption and lawlessness.

Going back to the garden of Eden, we see that the serpent's chief goal was to disrupt, divide, and destroy Adam and Eve's unity with God. They were no longer in agreement with God, and their relationship with Him died, just as a marriage can dissolve and die because of disagreement and disharmony. The enemy's primary strategy is to divide and conquer. The Lord Jesus said in Matthew 12:25, "Every… house divided against itself cannot stand." Our adversary, the devil, knows that. After Adam sinned, mankind no longer had dominion over the earth or even himself. Now it is reversed. Now mankind is a slave instead of a superior.

Man's Separation from Life

And the LORD God commanded the man, saying,
"Of every tree of the garden you may freely eat;
but of the tree of the knowledge of good and
evil you shall not eat, for in the day that
you eat of it you shall surely die."
(Genesi. 2:16–17)

You will recall that we talked about a more accurate rendering of "you shall surely die" being "dying you shall die." The minute we are born, we are in the process of dying until we are dead.

Let's go back to the original sin. Here is Genesis 3:1–7 again:

Now the serpent was more cunning than any beast of the field which the Lord God had made. And he said to the woman, "Has God indeed said, 'You shall not eat of every tree of the garden'?"

And the woman said to the serpent, "We may eat the fruit of the trees of the garden; but of the fruit of the tree which is in the midst of the garden, God has said, 'You shall not eat it, nor shall you touch it, lest you die.'"

Then the serpent said to the woman, "You will not surely die. For God knows that in the day you eat of it your eyes will be opened, and you will be like God, knowing good and evil."

So when the woman saw that the tree was good for food, that it was pleasant to the eyes, and a tree desirable to make one wise, she took of its fruit and ate. She also gave to her husband with her, and he ate. Then the eyes of both of them were opened, and they knew that they were

*naked; and they sewed fig leaves together and
made themselves coverings.*

Notice that the first seed of doubt the enemy attempted to sow into the mind of Eve was, "Did God really say that? Are you sure you heard Him right? Is that what He really meant?" When she responds in the affirmative, the serpent steps up the attack by flatly stating, "You will not surely die. God is not telling you the whole truth because He doesn't want you to know what He knows." However, what the serpent doesn't tell her is, "and for good reason." He is suggesting to Eve that God is not being honest with her, that He's withholding something from her that she should have, and that she cannot trust Him.

As soon as the adversary began to sow seeds of doubt into her mind regarding the word that God had given them, Eve should have refused to engage with him. We need to refuse to engage in any dialogue that calls into question the word of God—and get out of there. Our adversary is way too smart for us. He is too cunning for us to try to match his wits.

Unfortunately, Eve did not do that, and now she really fixes her gaze upon that tree that God told her, through her husband, not to touch. We might imagine her thinking, "That fruit looks really good. As a matter fact, probably better than any of the fruit of the other trees in this garden. I bet it tastes better than any of the fruit of the other trees." And the clincher is that it's brain food. Again, we might imagine her thinking, "I could be as smart as God. In fact, I could be my own god." And so, she ate and swallowed the lie of the serpent, and then gave some to her husband with her, and he ate and swallowed the lie of the serpent.

Adam, her husband, was with her! What was up with Adam? Why didn't he immediately put a stop to it, and tell Eve, "We're not going to listen to that. We're going to listen to God, and this isn't Him talking to us." Maybe he did—we don't really know. What we do know is that God said to Adam in Genesis 3:17, "because you listened to your wife" (NIV). Adam had a choice to make: whose voice was he going to listen to? Whose voice are we going to listen to?

This is what the Lord Jesus meant when He said in Luke 14:26, "If anyone comes to Me and does not hate his father and mother, wife and children, brothers and sisters, yes, and his own life also, he cannot be My disciple." He is not saying that we hate them for who they are, but we hate them in the sense that we refuse to listen to them if what they say does not agree with what God is saying. If their will is contrary to the will of God; if what they want for us is contrary to what God wants for us. Shortly after I became a born-again Christian, I refused to attend my mother's traditional church. I knew God wanted me to continue attending the spirit-filled church I had found. My own dear mother responded, "You must hate me."

The Lord Jesus put it in even stronger terms in Matthew 16:21–23 when He was speaking of his impending death.

From that time Jesus began to show to His disciples that He must go to Jerusalem, and suffer many things from the elders and chief priests and scribes, and be killed, and be raised the third day.

Then Peter took Him aside and began to rebuke Him, saying, "Far be it from You, Lord; this shall not happen to You!"

But He turned and said to Peter, "Get behind Me, Satan! You are an offense to Me, for you are not mindful of the things of God, but the things of men."

Peter was perhaps saying what anyone of us would say from a human standpoint. In essence he was saying, "We've left everything to follow You, and now You're telling us they're going to kill You? No way, we're not going to let that happen. We don't want a dead Messiah." Apparently, they either didn't hear the last part of what He said to them—"and be raised the third day"—or it was beyond their natural ability to grasp it.

Their concept of the Messiah's mission was a natural concept based on human reasoning. The Roman government was oppressing them, and they hoped this Messiah would free them. What they didn't understand was the greater oppression of their sin nature that would ultimately forever separate them from the Father, unless there was a Sin-Bearer to intervene on their behalf. A Mediator, who would negotiate their freedom from the penalty of sin—eternal death—with His own death.

Once again, here the serpent—the adversary, the devil—was seeking to deceive Jesus's disciples into believing they were right in their line of reasoning. However, the Lord Jesus exposed the adversary's attempt to do so by speaking directly to him who was speaking through Peter, "Get behind Me, Satan…you are not mindful of the things of God, but the things of men" (Matt. 16:23)

Adam and Eve not listening to the voice of the One who created them had consequences. As quoted earlier, here again we read Genesis 3:22–24:

> *Then the LORD God said, "Behold, the man has become like one of Us, to know good and evil. And now, lest he put out his hand and take also of the tree of life, and eat, and live forever"—therefore the LORD God sent him out of the garden of Eden to till the ground from which he was taken. So He drove out the man; and He placed cherubim at the east of the garden of Eden, and a flaming sword which turned every way, to guard the way to the tree of life.*

God had fully intended for the man and woman to eat from the Tree of Life and live forever together with Him, the Life-Giver, in a state of eternal life, peace, and joy. But not now. Death entered in and spoiled it all. Now they were separated from God and no longer had the hope of eternal life.

Romans 5:12 says, " Therefore, just as through one man sin entered the world, and death through sin, and thus death spread to all men, because all sinned." The death principle came into the world that God created. Now everyone and everything that God created was destined to die.

> *Nevertheless death reigned from Adam to Moses,*
> *even over those who had not sinned according to*
> *the likeness of the transgression of Adam, who is*
> *a type of Him who was to come. But the free gift is*
> *not like the offense. For if by the one man's offense*
> *many died, much more the grace of God and the*
> *gift by the grace of the one Man, Jesus Christ,*
> *abounded to many. And the gift is not like that*
> *which came through the one who sinned. For the*
> *judgment which came from one offense resulted in*
> *condemnation, but the free gift which came from*
> *many offenses resulted in justification. For if by the*
> *one man's offense death reigned through the one,*
> *much more those who receive abundance of grace*
> *and of the gift of righteousness will reign in life*
> *through the One, Jesus Christ.*
> (Rom. 5:14–17)

One man's sin, one man's offense, and Romans 5:19 goes on to say, "one man's disobedience." Just think about it, one wrong choice can have far-reaching consequences. "For the creation was subjected to futility, not willingly, but because of Him who subjected it in hope" (Romans 8:20). The whole of God's creation was spoiled, soiled, stained, and doomed to decay until death. A simple definition of death is the absence of life, just as darkness is the absence of light.

Romans 8:19 says, "For the earnest expectation of the creation eagerly waits for the revealing of the sons of God." Those who have been reunited with God, and God with them, through the intervention of the Mediator, the Son of God. Romans 8:21 says, "because the creation itself also will be delivered from the bondage of corruption into the glorious liberty of the children of God." God and man will be back together again. However, Romans 8:22 goes on to say that in the meantime **the whole creation** groans and labors with birth pangs.

Man's Separation from Man

And in the process of time it came to pass that Cain brought an offering of the fruit of the ground to the LORD. Abel also brought of the firstborn of his flock and of their fat. And the LORD respected Abel and his offering, but He did not respect Cain and his offering. And Cain was very angry, and his countenance fell.

So the LORD said to Cain, "Why are you angry? And why has your countenance fallen? If you do well, will you not be accepted? And if you do not do well, sin lies at the door. And its desire is for you, but you should rule over it."

Now Cain talked with Abel his brother; and it came
to pass, when they were in the field, that Cain rose
up against Abel his brother and killed him.
(Gen. 4:3–8)

Here is the first instance of the death principle at work, and it certainly wouldn't be the last of that principle separating mankind from one another.

Why do you think that God did not respect or receive Cain's offering? I think we get a clue from verse five. Cain became very angry and depressed. What was fueling his anger and depression? Proverbs 29:23 says that a man's (or a woman's) **pride** will bring him (or her) low (down). Proverbs 16:18 says, "Pride goes before destruction, and a haughty spirit before a fall."

Cain brought the fruit of his own labor to God as an offering, that which he had produced. Abel brought the fruit of God's labor as an offering to God to honor Him, that which God had produced. Cain believed that God should honor **him** for what **he** had produced. He was proud of what he had produced, and his pride was wounded. That wounded pride in Cain spawned a jealousy that ultimately resulted in the murder of his brother Abel.

This may be a hard word, but not only must pride be wounded, if we're ever going to be received by God or receive anything from God, it must be killed. 1 Peter 5:5 says in part, "God resists the proud, but gives grace to the humble."

Cain's brother Abel humbly offered to the Lord, in a prophetic sense, a blood sacrifice as a covering for sin. This offering foreshadowed the whole system of atonement for sin, which culminated in the blood sacrifice of Jesus, the Lamb of God. No sacrifice ever has to be made again!

The conflict between Cain and Abel reminds me of a similar conflict between the Jewish religious leaders and their Jewish "brother," the Lord Jesus. The religious leaders pridefully boasted in their works of keeping the law. However, the Lord Jesus calls them out on their hypocrisy in Matthew 23:4, "For they bind heavy burdens, hard to bear, and lay them on men's shoulders; but they themselves will not move them with one of their fingers." They kept people tied up with the burden of the law, with its rules and rituals, and had no sympathy or compassion whatsoever for the people themselves. The Lord Jesus goes on to call out their hypocrisy for 32 more verses to Matthew 23:36, ending up with a damming judgment upon them.

Therefore, indeed, I send you prophets,
wise men, and scribes: some of them you will kill
and crucify, and some of them you will scourge
in your synagogues and persecute from city
to city, that on you may come all the righteous
blood shed on the earth, from the blood of
righteous Abel to the blood of Zechariah,
son of Berechiah, whom you murdered
between the temple and the altar. Assuredly,

I say to you, all these things will come
upon this generation.
(Matt. 23:34–36)

As we suggested, going all the way back to the blood of righteous Abel in juxtaposition to the religious leaders of whom Jesus said, in Matthew 23:28, outwardly appeared righteous, but inwardly were "full of hypocrisy and lawlessness."

In Matthew 15:8, the Lord Jesus refers to Isaiah, who prophesied about the religious leaders of Jesus' day, that they honored God with their words, but their hearts were **far** from Him. Religion is based on law; a relationship is based on love. The religious leaders only had their performance of religious rituals, customs, and works of the law to support their claim of a knowledge of God. They had no relationship with the God they proclaimed and never would, as long as they maintained their claim to righteousness by the works of the law. In contrast, the apostle Paul states, in Philippians 3:9–10, his desire to "be found in Him, not having my own righteousness, which is from the law, but that which is through faith in Christ, the righteousness which is from God by faith; that I may know Him and the power of His resurrection, and the fellowship of His sufferings, being conformed to His death."

The Lord Jesus infuriated the religious leaders by calling them out on their hypocrisy and lack of true knowledge of God. Their fury ultimately reached its peak when they cried, "Crucify him!"

As we return to Cain and Abel, we see in Cain the first instance of the death principle at work, separating a man from a man. It all stemmed from pride. Pride is a killer. If it is not killed in us, it will kill us. This led to the death of Adam and Eve, and that death was passed on to all of humanity. Eve saw that the tree was able to make her wise, but with what kind of wisdom? 1 Corinthians 3:19 says that "the wisdom of this world is foolishness to God." We've all met at least one person with a prideful spirit regarding their knowledge.

Pride led to Lucifer's downfall. He said in essence, "I will ascend to the throne of the Most High and become God" (Isaiah 14:13–14). Pride led to the crucifixion of the Lord Jesus. The leaders had pride in their religious system and their control over the people. The Lord Jesus threatened that and their whole economy. This inspired their plot to kill Him. (John 12:19)

Death separates us from one another permanently in this life. It is the greatest fear, the greatest grief, and the greatest pain of all mankind. Hebrews 2:15 says in part, "Who through fear of death were all their lifetime subject to bondage."

Genesis 23:2 says, "So Sarah died…and Abraham came to mourn for Sarah and to weep for her." Abraham was grieved over his separation from Sarah. The Lord Jesus said of marriage, in Matthew 19:6, "What God has joined together, let not man separate." As mentioned earlier, the word used for *joined* in the Greek is akin to the term "super glue." It is meant to be permanent, and when broken by death, it can be excruciatingly painful, doing much damage.

> *And many of the Jews had joined the women around Martha and Mary, to comfort them concerning their brother.*
>
> *Then Martha, as soon as she heard that Jesus was coming, went and met Him, but Mary was sitting in the house. Now Martha said to Jesus, "Lord, if You had been here, my brother would not have died..."*
>
> *Then, when Mary came where Jesus was, and saw Him, she fell down at His feet, saying to Him, "Lord, if You had been here, my brother would not have died."*
>
> *Therefore, when Jesus saw her weeping, and the Jews who came with her weeping, He groaned in the spirit and was troubled. And He said, "Where have you laid him?"*
>
> *They said to Him, "Lord, come and see."*
>
> *Jesus wept.*
> (John 11:19–21, 32–35)

Here we see the depth of grief associated with the power of death to separate us from one another. "Lord, if You had just been here, our brother would still be here with us!" What is so striking and difficult about death is the finality of it. We can't help thinking about what could've been if they were still here with us. But our dead loved ones are gone, and they are not ever coming back.

King David sinned by taking another man's wife and impregnating her. He then added to that sin the sin of arranging for her husband's death. When he repented of his sin, he was forgiven, but the consequence was the death of the child born to him and Bathsheba. Regarding his child's death, David cried, "He shall not return to me." He was gone from this life, never to return. That is the horror of death. We were made to be social beings right from the beginning, when God said of Adam that it was not good for him to be alone and made a companion for him.

We were made for companionship, fellowship, and partnership—these three ships sailing together. As mentioned earlier, Genesis 1:27–28 tells us that God created them male and female and commanded them to be fruitful and multiply, filling the earth.

The Lord Jesus said in Matthew 16:18, "On this rock I will build My church." His church is a body of believers made up of many members intimately and intricately joined together. God never meant for us to be separated from one another by death. So the question is raised in John 11:37, "Could not this Man, who opened the eyes of the blind, also have kept [Lazarus] from dying?" Yes, He could have—for now—but the day would come when Lazarus would have died anyway. We needed a more permanent solution, and only the Mediator could negotiate that for us.

Chapter Three

The Reset

Then the LORD saw that the wickedness
of man was great in the earth, and that
every intent of the thoughts of his heart
was only evil continually.
(Gen. 6:5)

he wickedness of man was great. The Hebrew word for wickedness is *ra`* (rah).[12] It means bad, evil, unpleasant, giving pain, unhappiness, misery, sad, vicious in disposition, injury, adversity, distress, affliction. That is quite a list of negatives, all because of one decision to disobey the command of God.

As a result, the man and woman were cut off from God. They no longer had a consciousness of God. Their consciousness of God was taken captive by the evil one who deceived them into thinking they could be on the same

---

[12] Strong, James. "7451 רַע (*rah*)," Strong's Hebrew: 7451. רַע (*rah*) (Strong's Concordance, 2025), https://strongsconcordance.org/

level with God. The irony of it was that they were already like God—made in His image and likeness, pure and good, innocent, knowing no evil. They had no evil intentions or thoughts, and God intended them to keep it that way through His command to not eat from that tree.

However, when they disobeyed the command of God, their eyes were opened. They now had a consciousness of evil that caused them shame, guilt, and fear. They hid themselves from God. Their consciousness of God was overtaken by the consciousness of the evil, wicked nature of the one who deceived them. Now, when they wanted to do good, as the apostle Paul says in Romans 7:21, "evil is right there with me" (NIV). In fact, he goes on in verse 15, "For what I am doing, I do not understand. For what I will to do, that I do not practice; but what I hate, that I do." And in verses 22–24, "For I delight in the law of God according to the inward man. But I see another law in my members, warring against the law of my mind, and bringing me into captivity to the law of sin which is in my members. O wretched man that I am! Who will deliver me from this body of death?" Thank God, He provided a Deliverer, the Mediator who will negotiate that deliverance by His death on the cross.

The Lord God was sorry that He had made man and was grieved in His heart. Another way to interpret the Lord being grieved in His heart is that He had pain in His heart continually as He looked upon the people He had made. They now didn't look anything like Him. It is very much like parents who have children born to them and rear them with godly values and instruction, only to have them reject it all, preferring "all that is in the world—the lust of the flesh, the lust of the eyes, and the pride of life…" (1 John 2:16).

The Lord God was so grieved and pained in His heart over what He saw in those children He had created that He decided to wipe them all out and start all over again –

The Reset

How was God going to do this? Was he going to make man again out of the dust of the earth? No. Genesis 6:8 goes on to say, "But Noah found grace in the eyes of the Lord." Noah was a just man, perfect in his generation. Noah walked with God. Noah didn't live and walk according to the world in the lust of the flesh, and the lust of the eyes, and the pride of life. Noah was going to be God's man for the reset.

> *And God said to Noah, "The end of all flesh has come before Me, for the earth is filled with violence through them; and behold, I will destroy them with the earth. Make yourself an ark of gopherwood; make rooms in the ark, and cover it inside and outside with pitch. And this is how you shall make it: The length of the ark shall be three hundred cubits, its width fifty cubits, and its height thirty cubits. You shall make a window for the ark, and you shall finish it to a cubit from above; and set the door of the ark in its side. You shall make it*

with lower, second, and third decks. And behold,
I Myself am bringing floodwaters on the earth, to
destroy from under heaven all flesh in which is the
breath of life; everything that is on the earth shall
die. But I will establish My covenant with you;
and you shall go into the ark—you, your sons,
your wife, and your sons' wives with you. And of
every living thing of all flesh you shall bring two
of every sort into the ark, to keep them alive with
you; they shall be male and female. Of the birds
after their kind, of animals after their kind, and of
every creeping thing of the earth after its kind, two
of every kind will come to you to keep them alive.
And you shall take for yourself of all food that is
eaten, and you shall gather it to yourself; and it
shall be food for you and for them."

Thus Noah did; according to all that God
commanded him, so he did.
(Gen. 6:13–22)

God was going to start all over again with Noah, his wife, his three sons, and their wives. God decided to reset the earth by destroying every human being upon the face of the earth with a flood—every human being, that is, except for eight people. He revealed this to Noah and told him to prepare for it.

God not only commanded Noah to build an ark, but He taught him how to build it. This reminds me of another Man,

Christ Jesus, who said in John 12:49, "For I have not spoken on My own authority; but the Father who sent Me gave Me a command, what I should say and what I should speak."

God instructed Noah to build a three-story ark, 450 feet long, seventy-five feet wide, and forty-five feet high, with a capacity exceeding that of 500 railroad stock cars. Additionally, it was to be in the shape of a barge, making it difficult to capsize.

God told Noah that He would establish His covenant with him. This is the first mention of a biblical covenant. God engaged Noah in a covenantal agreement, saying in essence, "You, your sons, your wife, and your sons' wives go into the ark, and I will protect you."

The concept of covenant is an essential and fundamental theme throughout both the Old and New Testaments of the Bible. It speaks of the method by which God will bring heaven back to earth, and mankind back to God, and humanity back together with the abolishment of death.

The word *covenant* is used 292 times in the Bible. 250 of these instances are in the Old Testament. The Hebrew word for covenant is *briyth* (ber-eeth').[13] It means a compact or alliance between parties. It was often put into effect to resolve conflict and appease an offended party.[14] God later established a covenant with Abraham that he would be

---

[13] Strong, James. "1285 בְּרִית (*ber-eeth'*)," Strong's Hebrew: 1285. בְּרִית (*ber-eeth'*) (Strong's Concordance, 2025), https://strongsconcordance.org/

[14] Jack W. Hayford et al., *New Spirit-Filled Life Bible: New International Version* (Nashville: Thomas Nelson, 2015).

the father of a multitude and that God would be their God **forever**.

Covenant is one of the most theologically important words in the Bible. A ber-eeth may be made between individuals (such as a marriage covenant), between a king and his people, or by God and His people. All other Bible promises are based on this one leading up to the Mediator, Christ Jesus, who ensured that the promises of God are "yes, and in Him Amen" (2 Cor. 1:20).

> *But now He has obtained a more excellent ministry, inasmuch as He is also Mediator of a better covenant, which was established on better promises.*
>
> *For if that first covenant had been faultless, then no place would have been sought for a second. Because finding fault with them, He says: "Behold, the days are coming, says the LORD, when I will make a new covenant with the house of Israel and with the house of Judah—not according to the covenant that I made with their fathers in the day when I took them by the hand to lead them out of the land of Egypt; because they did not continue in My covenant, and I disregarded them, says the LORD. For this is the covenant that I will make with the house of Israel after those days, says the LORD: I will put My laws in their mind and write them on their hearts; and I will be their God, and*

they shall be My people. None of them shall teach his neighbor, and none his brother, saying, 'Know the Lord,' for all shall know Me, from the least of them to the greatest of them. For I will be merciful to their unrighteousness, and their sins and their lawless deeds I will remember no more."
(Heb. 8:6–12)

Again, this was all accomplished by the Mediator, the Lord Jesus, who said in Luke 22:20 to His disciples on the evening before His death, "This cup is the new covenant in My blood, which is shed for you."

The Greek word for covenant is *diatheke* (dee-ath-ay'-kay).[15] It means "an arrangement that requests validation."[16] In the Old Testament, covenants were normally validated, or guaranteed, by the shedding of blood. In Genesis 8:20, after Noah, his wife, his sons, and his sons' wives came out of the ark, Noah built an altar of sacrifice unto the Lord, upon which he offered slain, clean animals and birds as a burnt offering unto the Lord. This ordinance would continue and be refined to become the covenant by which God would pardon sin. The forgiveness of sin would always require the shedding of the blood of innocent animals. As Hebrews 9:22 states, "And according to the law almost all things are

---

[15] Strong, James. "1242 διαθήκη (*dee-ath-ay'-kay*)" Strong's Greek: 1242. διαθήκη (*dee-ath-ay'-kay*) (Strong's Concordance, 2025), https://strongsconcordance.org/
[16] Jack W. Hayford et al., *New Spirit-Filled Life Bible: New International Version* (Nashville: Thomas Nelson, 2015).

purified with blood, and without shedding of blood there is no remission." The innocent for the guilty.

Noah did everything God commanded him to do and how it was to be done. Historians believe it took anywhere from fifty-five to seventy-five years for Noah to build such an enormous ark. I can only imagine that there must've been times Noah thought, "Why am I doing this? It doesn't look like rain, and it doesn't really rain here much." However, that's what true faith is all about. It rests solely on what God has said and should always be related to what He has already said in His word, the Bible. It does not depend on what it looks like or what is reasonable. True faith is not reasonable, nor does it depend on reason. True faith comes, as Romans 10:17 says, "by hearing, and hearing by the word of God."

Hebrews 11:1 says that "faith is the substance of things hoped for, the evidence of things not seen." Hebrews 11:6 goes on to say, "without faith it is impossible to please Him, for he who comes to God must believe that He is, and that He is a rewarder of those who diligently seek Him." Faith supported by diligence, which means to see through to completion, is a rewarding combination. Hebrews 11:7 recognizes Noah's faithful obedience to God's command, saying that he was "divinely warned of things not yet seen, moved with godly fear, [and] prepared an ark for the saving of his household, by which he condemned the world and became heir of the righteousness which is according to faith." Can you imagine it? Noah spent fifty-five to seventy-five years of his life building a boat for something he had **not yet seen**.

However, the glory of it was that sooner or later he would see it, maintaining his faith in the God who "calls those things which do not exist as though they did" (Romans 4:17).

In addition to that, we must consider the fact that the boat wasn't ready yet. It still had to be prepared for the enormity of what was to come. The same is true for us. God must prepare us, build us up to the measure of what he has prepared for us. Joseph was not prepared for the magnitude of the dreams God had revealed to him. He had to go through a time of preparation, and the preparation was not pleasant. It was rigorous, bringing him to a place of complete and total obedience to God. His obedience had to be more than lip service. Joseph had to be tested and his obedience to God proven before he could be moved into what God had prepared for him.

At times, we may wonder why we must go through difficulties. I believe the first reason is that we live in a troubled world. However, we can take heart in the fact that whatever we go through must first be approved by the Most High God. If He approves it, our troubles will prepare us for what He plans to do in our lives. We will not be slaves and captives to the troubles of this world. They will be our servants to make us overcomers, to make us more like our ultimate Overcomer, the Lord Jesus. And through the hardships, we will be prepared for every good work that

God has for us. Whatever that work is, big or small, we will be made fit for it.

Genesis 6:22 says that Noah did according to **all** that God commanded him—for fifty-five to seventy-five years! And the day finally came when God said to Noah, "Come into the ark, you and all your household, because **I have seen** that you are righteous before me in this generation."

I believe there are times that God is waiting to see something in us during times of testing and proving. He is waiting to see whether there will be a manifestation, a demonstration of our declaration. You've heard the sayings, "Talk is cheap," and "Actions speak louder than words." What good is what I say if I'm not willing to back it up by what I do? John 3:16 says in part, "God so loved the world that He *gave* His only begotten Son" (emphasis added). What good would that word be if the Son was not willing to be given. In fact, we see the incredible weight and trauma of this decision in the garden of Gethsemane.

> *Then they came to a place which was named Gethsemane; and He said to His disciples, "Sit here while I pray." And He took Peter, James, and John with Him, and He began to be troubled and deeply distressed. Then He said to them, "My soul is exceedingly sorrowful, even to death. Stay here and watch." He went a little farther, and fell on the ground, and prayed that if it were possible, the hour might pass from*

Him. And He said, "Abba, Father, all things are
possible for You. Take this cup away from Me;
nevertheless, not what I will, but what You will."
(Mark 14:32–36)

He was troubled and deeply distressed. Have you ever been troubled or deeply distressed? His soul was exceedingly sorrowful, even to death. To me that could mean that the Lord Jesus was in such agony that He wanted to die. Have you ever been in such agony that you wished you could die? Jesus, our great High Priest, knows all about it. In fact, in Luke's account of the Lord Jesus in the garden of Gethsemane, he says that the Lord Jesus was in such agony that he began to sweat, and his sweat became like great drops of blood falling to the ground. He was already bleeding for us before He even got to the cross.

Another point to be made here is that the Lord Jesus declared to the Father, "all things are possible for You. Take this cup from Me." Have you yet discovered that God does not always do what He's able to do? If He doesn't do what He's able to do, it's because He has something else in mind. The Father could've delivered His beloved Son from such horror and agony of the cross, but then He would've only saved His beloved Son, and not all of us. He didn't send his Son to be saved. He sent his Son to be sacrificed so that we could be saved.

You shall take with you seven each of every clean
animal, a male and his female; two each of animals

that are unclean, a male and his female; also seven
each of birds of the air, male and female, to keep
the species alive on the face of all the earth.
(Gen. 7:2–3)

Not only did God save Noah and his household from the flood, but He saved a male and female of every clean and unclean animal and birds of the air.

In the six hundredth year of Noah's life, in the
second month, the seventeenth day of the month,
on that day all the fountains of the great deep
were broken up, and the windows of heaven were
opened. And the rain was on the earth forty days
and forty nights.

On the very same day Noah and Noah's sons,
Shem, Ham, and Japheth, and Noah's wife and
the three wives of his sons with them, entered the
ark—they and every beast after its kind, all cattle
after their kind, every creeping thing that creeps
on the earth after its kind, and every bird after
its kind, every bird of every sort. And they went
into the ark to Noah, two by two, of all flesh in
which is the breath of life. So those that entered,
male and female of all flesh, went in as God had
commanded him; and the LORD shut him in.
(Gen. 7:11–16)

Not only did rain come down from the sky, the heavens, forty days and forty nights, but water also burst up from the ground to flood the earth. However, verse 16 says that the Lord "shut him in." I personally believe that not only did the Lord shut him in and shelter him, but He also went in with him.

The Ark of the Covenant was an extremely important symbol in Old Testament times. It represented God's presence with the Israelites. They knew that as long as God was with them, then His protection and provision would also be with them.

> *God is our refuge and strength,*
> *A very present help in trouble.*
> *Therefore we will not fear,*
> *Even though the earth be removed,*
> *And though the mountains be carried into the*
> *midst of the sea;*
> *Though its waters roar and be troubled,*
> *Though the mountains shake with its swelling.*
> *Selah…*
>
> *God is in the midst of her, she shall not be moved;*
> *God shall help her, just at the break of dawn.*
> (Ps. 46:1–3, 5)

His very presence helps us in the time of our trouble so that we are not overcome by the trouble. In His presence, the trouble doesn't affect us. The Lord Jesus said in John

14:1, "Let *not* your *heart* be troubled; you believe in God, believe also in Me" (emphasis added).

> *Now when He got into a boat, His disciples*
> *followed Him. And suddenly a great tempest arose*
> *on the sea, so that the boat was covered with the*
> *waves. But He was asleep. Then His disciples*
> *came to Him and awoke Him, saying, "Lord, save*
> *us! We are perishing!"*
>
> *But He said to them, "Why are you fearful, O you*
> *of little faith?" Then He arose and rebuked the*
> *winds and the sea, and there was a great calm.*
> (Matthew 8:23–26)

Have you ever had a "sudden tempest" arise in your life? An unexpected storm of trouble coming out of nowhere? Not only that, but it seemed like the Lord Jesus was asleep in the midst of it. *He's not doing anything, and it's getting worse!* "Lord, get up and do something; we're going to drown!"

And so, the Lord Jesus got up at their urgent, desperate request and rebuked the wind and waves, and "there was a great calm." However, before He did that, He rebuked them for having such little faith. The presence of the King of Kings, the Lord of Lords, the Great I Am was in their boat, and as long as He was, that boat was not going down. They are **not** going to perish! Real faith in Jesus is when I trust Him to take me through the storm, rather than keeping me from it, even if He is asleep in my boat. My faith in him will never grow if He always keeps me **from** the storm; my faith in Him grows when I find Him keeping me **in** the storm. The greater calm I need is the calm **inside** of me during the storm **outside** of me—that same calm that the Lord Jesus had when He was fast asleep in the bottom of the boat in the midst of the storm. And that has been given to us by the Lord Jesus. As He said in John 14:27, "Peace I leave with you, My peace I give to you." He wants to give us the same peace that He has, the same peace that enabled Him to sleep in a storm." He then goes on to repeat what He said in verse one of the same chapter; "Let not your heart be troubled, neither let it be afraid."

The Greek word for heart that the Lord Jesus used is *kardia* (kar-dee'-ah).[17] It is the center and seat of spiritual life.[18] The core of the mind. The fountain of thoughts, passions, emotions, desires, appetites, affections, purposes, endeavors. It is the foundation of understanding. The nucleus of the will, character, and decisions. It is the fulcrum of the soul, as far as it is affected and stirred in a good or bad way. Just as the physical organ of the heart is in the center of our bodies and distributes the blood to the body, so too does our spiritual heart distribute lifeblood to our spiritual being—peace or anxiety, love or fear, faith or doubt, calm or distress.

---

[17] Strong, James. "2588 καρδία (*kar-dee'-ah*)" Strong's Greek: 2588. καρδία (*kar-dee'-ah*) (Strong's Concordance, 2025), https://strongsconcordance.org/
[18] Jack W. Hayford et al., *New Spirit-Filled Life Bible: New International Version* (Nashville: Thomas Nelson, 2015).

The Lord God shut Noah and his household into the ark of His presence, safe from the flood that would cover the earth. God decided to rid the earth of evil and unrighteous humanity, to start all over again with one righteous man, Noah. Again, He intended to bring heaven back to earth, reconcile humanity with Himself, and end the separation of mankind by death. However, the nature of the first Adam was still in Noah. This sin nature had the potential to cause his righteousness to fail. Noah was a foreshadowing of the righteousness that would come from God through His only begotten Son, Jesus. His righteousness would not fail, but would prevail in bringing heaven back to earth, humanity back to God, and mankind to one another. The Lord Jesus was the embodiment of heaven and earth and heaven on earth.

So God blessed Noah and his sons, and said to them: "Be fruitful and multiply, and fill the earth. And the fear of you and the dread of you shall be on every beast of the earth, on every bird of the air, on all that move on the earth, and on all the fish of the sea. They are given into your hand. Every moving thing that lives shall be food for you. I have given you all things, even as the green herbs.
(Gen. 9:1–3)

And so, the reset begins. "Be fruitful and multiply, and fill the earth." The same words He said to Adam and Eve in the beginning. He gave Noah dominion over all life upon the earth just as He gave to Adam in the beginning. He gave him every moving thing for food in addition to what grows up from the ground. God was now giving them meat for food—something He hadn't allowed Adam in the beginning.

God goes on to say to Noah and his sons in Genesis 9:9–11 that never again shall there be a flood to destroy the earth. What is interesting to note here is that God is not saying that He would never destroy the earth again. He is saying He would never destroy the earth with a **flood** again. This is important to distinguish in light of what we read in 2 Peter.

> *For this they willfully forget: that by the word of God the heavens were of old, and the earth standing out of water and in the water, by which the world that then existed perished, being flooded with water. But the heavens and the earth which are now preserved by the same word, are reserved for fire until the day of judgment and perdition of ungodly men.*
> (2 Pet. 3:5–7)

A few verses later, we read:

> *But the day of the Lord will come as a thief in the night, in which the heavens will pass away with a great noise, and the elements will melt with fervent heat; both the earth and the works that are in it will be burned up.*
> (2 Pet. 3:10)

Peter continues in verse 13, "Nevertheless we, according to His promise, look for new heavens and a new earth in which righteousness dwells." This will be the ultimate reset that will forever remain.

> *And Noah began to be a farmer, and he planted a vineyard. Then he drank of the wine and was drunk, and became uncovered in his tent. And Ham, the father of Canaan, saw the nakedness of his father, and told his two brothers outside. But Shem and Japheth took a garment, laid it on both their shoulders, and went backward and covered the nakedness of their father. Their faces were turned away, and they did not see their father's nakedness.*
>
> *So Noah awoke from his wine, and knew what his younger son had done to him. Then he said:*
>
> *"Cursed be Canaan;*
> *A servant of servants*
> *He shall be to his brethren."*
> (Gen. 9:20–25)

In a striking similarity to Adam's nakedness in the garden, Noah became uncovered in his tent. What he had done was exposed by his son, Ham, who saw it and told his brothers. They then took a garment and covered up their father's shame. This is very similar to Adam and Eve's shameful exposure of their nakedness because they ate from the Tree of the Knowledge of Good and Evil. They tried to cover their shame with fig leaves.

Noah curses his son Ham for exposing him, and ultimately, that cursing would have an effect on mankind going forward. Again, this is like God cursing the ground as a judgment upon Adam for his disobedience. "Cursed is the ground for your sake; in toil you shall eat of it all the days of your life. Both thorns and thistles it shall bring forth for you" (Gen. 3:17–18). The ground is not going to be very cooperative with the man's efforts to bring forth food from it. "In the sweat of your face you shall eat bread till you return to the ground" (Gen. 3:19).

It's no wonder we're tired when we come home from work. The stress and strain of it, and the toll it takes on us mentally and physically, all resulted from one man's decision to disobey the command of God.

Thank God that He had another Man, His only begotten Son, Jesus, who would fully obey every command of the Father. His obedient life was offered in exchange for our disobedient life and the stressful, fatal consequences thereof. Now we can have the favor of God to help us with the unfavorable. Now we can have rest from our labor, as the Lord Jesus said in Matthew 11:28. Now we have the ultimate hope of eternal life with Him, where there will be no more sweat and no more toil and no more death!

Going back to Noah, the reset has not taken. Ham exposed the shame of his nakedness, related to his drunkenness. Ham's two brothers tried to cover it up with a garment.

However, when Noah sobered up, he knew what Ham had done and cursed him. So, even though God started all over again with one righteous man, He was still working with the same material prone to the same unrighteousness.

The Rising

Now the Lord had said to Abram:

> *"Get out of your country,*
> *From your family*
> *And from your father's house,*
> *To a land that I will show you.*
> *I will make you a great nation;*
> *I will bless you*
> *And make your name great;*
> *And you shall be a blessing.*
> *I will bless those who bless you,*
> *And I will curse him who curses you;*
> *And in you all the families of the earth shall be*
> *blessed."*
> (Gen. 12:1–3)

In order for there to be a *rising* of the people of God, a man is going to have to be willing to obey God. He will have to leave his family, his home, and all that is familiar to him and go where he's never gone before. This is true in our own lives. If we are ever going to rise to the level that God has for us, we need to be willing to leave our current circumstances.

We need to be willing to get out of our comfort zone. We need to be willing to leave what is familiar, what is predictable, and venture into the unfamiliar, the unpredictable. We have to decide whether we just want to stay where we are and be comfortable, or go to where God is leading us and be willing to bear the discomfort and unfamiliarity of it.

The rising has to do with growth. I can't grow if I don't go. The Lord Jesus said to His disciples, just before He went back to heaven, in Matthew 28:19 "*Go* therefore and make disciples of *all* the nations" (emphasis added). Mark 16:15 says, "Go into *all* the world and preach the gospel to every creature" (emphasis added). The kingdom of God would never have grown if the disciples didn't go. The people of God can't grow if they don't go.

However, we will not go it alone. The very last verse of Matthew's gospel says, "And lo, *I am with you always*, even to the end of the age" (Matt. 28:20, emphasis added).

> *And the LORD said to Abram, after Lot had*
> *separated from him: "Lift your eyes now*
> *and look from the place where you are—*
> *northward, southward, eastward, and westward;*
> *for all the land which you see I give to you and*
> *your descendants forever. And I will make*
> *your descendants as the dust of the earth;*
> *so that if a man could number the dust of*
> *the earth, then your descendants also could be*

> *numbered. Arise, walk in the land through*
> *its length and its width, for I give it to you."*
> (Gen. 13:14-17)

Lift your eyes now and look up from where you are. If there is ever going to be a rising to greater heights in our journey with the Lord, there will have to be a lifting, a lifting of our vision beyond where we are. Our relationship with the Lord is a journey, which means it is not stationary, but mobile. Again, God said to Abraham, "Arise, walk in the land through its length and its width, for I give it to you." There is more ground to be gained and territory to be taken as we move ever closer to our final destination, increasing the number of travelers we bring with us along the way. Ephesians 4:13 says, "till we all come to the unity of the faith and of the knowledge of the Son of God, to a perfect man, to the measure of the stature of the fullness of Christ." We are made ready to be added to the great cloud of witnesses who have gone before us, as mentioned in Hebrews 12:1, to live forever with the King of Kings and Lord of Lords!

> *After these things the word of the LORD came to*
> *Abram in a vision, saying, "Do not be afraid,*
> *Abram. I am your shield, your exceedingly great*
> *reward."*
>
> *But Abram said, "Lord GOD, what will You give*
> *me, seeing I go childless, and the heir of my house*

*is Eliezer of Damascus?" Then Abram said,
"Look, You have given me no offspring; indeed
one born in my house is my heir!"*

*And behold, the word of the LORD came to him,
saying, "This one shall not be your heir, but one
who will come from your own body shall be your
heir." Then He brought him outside and said,
"Look now toward heaven, and count the stars
if you are able to number them." And He said to
him, "So shall your descendants be."*

*And he believed in the LORD, and He accounted it
to him for righteousness.*
(Gen. 15:1–6)

Abram was childless at the age of seventy-five, and yet God said to him that one who will come from his own body would be his heir, and from him would come countless numbers of descendants. Then it tells us that Abram believed God. That was the key to releasing the promise of God—**believing** what He says. That is the key to releasing all the promises of God to us—believing Him and believing **in** Him. This is the key to being righteous in the sight of God—not our own righteousness, but faith in Him who is righteous, and that is counted as righteousness unto us.

*But to him who does not work but believes on Him
who justifies the ungodly, his faith is accounted*

*for righteousness, just as David also describes
the blessedness of the man to whom God imputes
righteousness apart from works:*

*"Blessed are those whose lawless deeds are forgiven,
And whose sins are covered;
Blessed is the man to whom the* LORD *shall not
impute sin."*
(Rom. 4:5–8)

There is no way we can justify our lawless deeds, our sin, by our own works; I may fast, I may read my Bible more, I may go to the house of worship more. That won't justify me, because I'll sin again, and again, and again. The only thing that will justify me is acknowledging my sin and sinfulness and crying out to God for forgiveness. We must have faith in Him alone, and He will cover our sin. That covering is His blood.

The Bible says, "The soul who sins shall die (Ezek. 18:20a). If that is the case, then I am a dead man, forever separated from the Author and Giver of Life. The only hope I have is for one willing to die in my place. However, first, who would be willing to do that? Romans 5:7 says that no one would likely die for a righteous person and there's a slight chance someone might die for a good person. I am a sinner, so I'm neither righteous nor good.

Second, where would we find a qualified candidate to die in our place, since we are all in the same condition? Romans 3:23 says, "All have sinned and fall short of the glory of God." There was only one who qualified, the

Mediator, Christ Jesus. Romans 5:8 says in part, "while we were still sinners, Christ died for us." He was conceived in the womb of the Virgin Mary and born without the sinful Adamic nature so that He could mediate our justification to the Father through His death.

> *When Abram was ninety-nine years old, the LORD appeared to Abram and said to him, "I am Almighty God; walk before Me and be blameless. And I will make My covenant between Me and you, and will multiply you exceedingly." Then Abram fell on his face, and God talked with him, saying: "As for Me, behold, My covenant is with you, and you shall be a father of many nations. No longer shall your name be called Abram, but your name shall be Abraham; for I have made you a father of many nations. I will make you exceedingly fruitful; and I will make nations of you, and kings shall come from you.*
> (Gen. 17:1–6)

And so the rising is going to come from one man Abram, which means "exalted father."[19] However, Abram will now be called Abraham, which means "father of a multitude."[20] All of this serves as foreshadowing God bringing heaven

---

[19] Strong, James. "87 אַבְרָם (ab-rawm')," Strong's Hebrew: 87. אַבְרָם (ab-rawm') (Strong's Concordance, 2025), https://strongsconcordance.org/

[20] Strong, James. "85 אַבְרָהָם (ab-raw-hawm')," Strong's Hebrew: 85. אַבְרָהָם (ab-raw-hawm') (Strong's Concordance, 2025), https://strongsconcordance.org/

back to earth and mankind back to God as the people of God living according to the will and commands of God. It is also a foreshadowing of the Man, God's only begotten Son, whom He would give to the world that "whoever believes in Him should not perish but have everlasting life" (John 3:16). This Man would have a people against whom the gates of hell would not prevail (Matt. 16:18). A people made in his own image and likeness, filled with the same Spirit that raised the Lord Jesus from the dead. As we are filled with the Spirit, He makes us alive unto God and dead to sin.

A primary purpose for God is to make us like the Son. As Romans 8:28–29 says, "And we know that all things work together for good to those who love God, to those who are the called according to His purpose. For whom He foreknew, He also predestined to be conformed to the image of His Son, that He might be the firstborn among many brethren." God is able to make **all** things work together for good. What good? To be made like the Son who is, as Hebrews 1:3 says, "the express image of His person." This was God's purpose right from the very beginning—to have children who would bear His image upon the earth He created. Adam lost that image in the garden of Eden through the trickery of the serpent. Therefore, heaven was separated from earth and mankind from God. However, God never abandoned his original purpose to have a people upon the earth who would bear His image and likeness and with whom He would dwell.

Then God said to Abraham, "As for Sarai your wife, you shall not call her name Sarai, but Sarah shall be her name. And I will bless her and also give you a son by her; then I will bless her, and she shall be a mother of nations; kings of peoples shall be from her."

Then Abraham fell on his face and laughed, and said in his heart, "Shall a child be born to a man who is one hundred years old? And shall Sarah, who is ninety years old, bear a child?" And Abraham said to God, "Oh, that Ishmael might live before You!"

Then God said: "No, Sarah your wife shall bear you a son, and you shall call his name Isaac; I will establish My covenant with him for an everlasting covenant, and with his descendants after him.
(Gen. 17:15–19)

God changed Abraham's wife's name from *Sarai* to *Sarah*. Interestingly, both names mean "a princess."[21] However, the name Sarah has a much stronger connotation, as we see in verse 16 where God says that she will be a **mother** of nations. The name Sarai is a description of her character. The name Sarah is a description of her purpose, to be the mother of nations. And this will come directly

---

[21] Jack W. Hayford et al., *New Spirit-Filled Life Bible: New International Version* (Nashville: Thomas Nelson, 2015).

by the hand of God, for Sarah is barren and well past childbearing age at ninety years old. Her husband is 100 years old and well past the age of potency. However, God is not at all limited by these factors. There is going to be a rising of peoples and nations upon the earth by the hand of God through one man and one woman who could never accomplish it by natural means.

> *Then the LORD appeared to him by the terebinth trees of Mamre, as he was sitting in the tent door in the heat of the day. So he lifted his eyes and looked, and behold, three men were standing by him; and when he saw them, he ran from the tent door to meet them, and bowed himself to the ground.*
> (Gen. 18:1–2)

The Lord appears to Abraham, and when he "looks up," he sees three men standing by him, and he bows down to the ground. The word for Lord in Hebrew is Yahweh, so it is the Lord God, Himself, who appears to Abraham.[22] What is interesting to note here is that the appearance of Yahweh is immediately followed by the appearance of three men. It begs the question, is Abraham granted the amazing vision of seeing God in three persons—Father, Son, and Holy Spirit—in human form?

---

[22] Jack W. Hayford et al., *New Spirit-Filled Life Bible: New International Version* (Nashville: Thomas Nelson, 2015).

In the beginning, God created the heavens and the earth and everything in them. After that, Genesis 1:26 says, "Then *God* said, 'Let *Us* make man in *Our* image, according to *Our* likeness'" (emphasis added). So, here we have God referring to himself as *us*.

The Lord Jesus said to his eleven disciples in Matthew 28:19, "Go therefore and make disciples of all the nations, baptizing them in the name of the Father and of the Son and of the Holy Spirit."

The Lord Jesus also said in John 14:9, "He who has seen Me has seen the Father." Luke 3:22 tells us that when Jesus was baptized in the Jordan river, "the Holy Spirit descended in bodily form like a dove upon Him." So, here we see God the Father, God the Son, and God the Holy Spirit in one Man, Christ Jesus.

> *Then they said to him,*
> *"Where is Sarah your wife?"*
>
> *So he said, "Here, in the tent."*
>
> *And He said, "I will certainly return to you according to the time of life, and behold, Sarah your wife shall have a son."*
>
> *(Sarah was listening in the tent door which was behind him.) Now Abraham and Sarah were old, well advanced in age; and Sarah had passed the age of childbearing. Therefore Sarah laughed*

*within herself, saying, "After I have grown old,
shall I have pleasure, my lord being old also?"*

*And the LORD said to Abraham, "Why did Sarah
laugh, saying, 'Shall I surely bear a child, since I
am old?' Is anything too hard for the Lord? At the
appointed time I will return to you, according to
the time of life, and Sarah shall have a son."*

*But Sarah denied it, saying, "I did not laugh," for
she was afraid.*

And He said, "No, but you did laugh!"
(Gen. 18:9–15)

The triune God in the bodily form of these three men
have a message for Abraham's wife, Sarah. They are coming
back again, and when they do, Sarah will have a son. This
was totally out of the natural order of things. Both Abraham
and Sarah were "well advanced in age," and Sarah's ship
had long since sailed, so to speak. In fact, when Sarah heard
them say it, she laughed. To paraphrase her, she may have
thought, "You gotta be kiddin' me; ain't no way that's gonna
happen!" And the Lord said, "Why did Sarah laugh … Is
anything too hard for the Lord?" And to paraphrase the Lord,
He is saying, "Do you know who you're dealing with here?"

*"For as the rain comes down, and the snow
from heaven,
And do not return there,
But water the earth,*

And make it bring forth and bud,
That it may give seed to the sower
And bread to the eater.

So shall My word be that goes forth from
My mouth;
It shall not return to Me void,
But it shall accomplish what I please,
And it shall prosper in the thing for which I sent it.
(Isa. 55:10–11)

"So shall my word be." When God speaks, it is done. When God says, "Let there be light," there is light. Only God can make something out of nothing. He's going to do that with Sarah in His ongoing determination to have a people upon the earth that reflect His glory; the glory of heaven coming back to earth.

Chapter Four

The Release

*Now Moses was tending the flock of Jethro
his father-in-law, the priest of Midian.
And he led the flock to the back of the desert,
and came to Horeb, the mountain of God.
And the Angel of the LORD appeared to him
in a flame of fire from the midst of a bush.
So he looked, and behold, the bush was burning
with fire, but the bush was not consumed.
Then Moses said, "I will now turn aside and
see this great sight, why the bush does not burn."*

*So when the LORD saw that he turned aside to look,
God called to him from the midst of the bush and
said, "Moses, Moses!"*

And he said, "Here I am."

*Then He said, "Do not draw near this place.
Take your sandals off your feet, for the place
where you stand is holy ground." Moreover*

He said, "I am the God of your father—the God
of Abraham, the God of Isaac, and the God of
Jacob." And Moses hid his face, for he was afraid
to look upon God.

And the LORD *said: "I have surely seen the*
oppression of My people who are in Egypt, and
have heard their cry because of their taskmasters,
for I know their sorrows. So I have come down
to deliver them out of the hand of the Egyptians,
and to bring them up from that land to a good and
large land, to a land flowing with milk and honey,
to the place of the Canaanites and the Hittites and
the Amorites and the Perizzites and the Hivites
and the Jebusites. Now therefore, behold, the
cry of the children of Israel has come to Me, and
I have also seen the oppression with which the
Egyptians oppress them. Come now, therefore,
and I will send you to Pharaoh that you may bring
My people, the children of Israel, out of Egypt."
(Ex. 3:1–10)

*H*ere we see Moses tending sheep on the backside of the desert in relative obscurity. Previously, Moses was a Hebrew living in Egypt, where his people lived under the cruel oppression of Pharaoh, the king of Egypt. At the time of Moses's birth in Egypt, the king of Egypt had issued an edict to kill all the male children born to

Hebrew women because their vast numbers became a threat to the Egyptians. However, the midwives feared God and refused to do it. When Pharoah confronted them for not doing what he commanded, they said the Hebrew women were strong and gave birth before they arrived. So, Pharaoh commanded his people to cast every male child born to the Hebrews into the Nile River.

However, when Moses was born, his mother hid him for three months, and when she could hide him no longer, she put him in a basket and laid it in the reeds by the river's bank. Then the daughter of Pharaoh came down to bathe at the river and saw the basket among the reeds in the river. She sent her maid to get it. She then called for the baby's mother to nurse the child, and ultimately, Moses became the son of Pharaoh's daughter.

However, there came an occasion where Moses saw an Egyptian beating a fellow Hebrew and intervened, killing the Egyptian and burying him in the sand. The next day, Moses observed two Hebrew men fighting and, once again, intervened. When he did, one of the men asked him if he was going to kill him as he did the Egyptian. Moses was exposed and fled from Egypt to Midian. This was his location when the current passage took place.

Moses had been on the backside of the desert tending sheep for forty years before his encounter with the living God. What is the significance of the backside of the desert? It is a place where no one can see Moses. This raises the question, "What am I like when no one can see me?" Am

I the same whether people can see me or not? Or am I one thing in front of people and something else when no one is looking? Was Moses beating the sheep when no one was looking? Was he constantly complaining about having such a menial, unnoticed task after he had such visible prominence in Egypt?

In 1 Samuel 16, after the failure of Saul to obey the Lord's command, God charged the prophet Samuel with the task of choosing the next king of Israel. He directed Samuel to go to the house of Jesse, who had eight sons, and choose one of them. When Samuel saw Eliab, Jesse's firstborn son, he said, "Surely this must be the one," based on his impressive appearance and height. However, God immediately corrected him, saying, "Do not look at his appearance or at his physical stature, because I have refused him. For the LORD does not see as man sees; for man looks at the outward appearance, but the LORD looks at the heart" (1 Sam. 16:7). God looks at the inner person, the part that only He sees.

One by one, Jesse's sons appeared before Samuel, and each time the Lord said, "Nope, not this one." What was Samuel to do? He was quite sure the Lord had sent him to the house of Jesse. Finally, Samuel asked Jesse if he had any more sons. Jesse replied that the youngest, probably a teenager and small in stature, was out tending the sheep. Jesse didn't even think to invite him because he was seeing as mankind sees—what a person looks like rather than what they **are** like. Samuel immediately directed Jesse to send for him. As soon as he was brought in, the Lord said to Samuel, "Get up and anoint him. This is the one."

Moses faithfully tended sheep on the backside of the desert, alone, unseen for forty years. If he had any further aspirations of greatness, they were long gone by now. I would venture to say that was by God's design. God can't use a man or woman with aspirations for their own greatness. All of that must be put to death in us so that our only aspiration is to see God's greatness on display. The apostle Paul put it very succinctly in Galatians 2:20, "I have been crucified with Christ; it is no longer I who live, but Christ lives in me; and the life which I now live in the flesh I live by faith in the Son of God, who loved me and gave Himself for me."

After forty years on the backside of the desert, Moses's time had come. God revealed Himself to Moses and he revealed the task He had for him. The task the Great I Am had for him was to deliver His people Israel from the cruel bondage of the Egyptians. We must realize that the greater the task God has for us, the greater the preparation. That preparation may be long and rigorous. God entrusts a great task to one he can trust. Complete devotion to Him must be proven. God knows just the right proving ground for each one He calls. That proving ground for Moses was forty years of tending sheep in a place where he received no recognition or praise from others. However, God saw him there all forty of those years. God had his eye on him all forty of those years. At the appointed time, God's time, He let him know it.

This is an important lesson for us to learn in our journey with the Lord—His appointed time. Ecclesiastes 3:1 says, "To everything there is a season, a time for every purpose under heaven." God knows when it's time for a thing. And if God is taking his time bringing to pass the thing we are waiting for on the outside, it may be that there is work to be done on the inside before that thing comes on the outside. What I am is far more important than what I have. I will not be taking what I have into eternity, but if I am a child of God I will be taking who I am into eternity with the Great I Am.

> *And the Lord said: "I have surely seen the*
> *oppression of My people who are in Egypt,*
> *and have heard their cry because of their*
> *taskmasters, for I know their sorrows. So I have*
> *come down to deliver them out of the hand*
> *of the Egyptians, and to bring them up from*
> *that land to a good and large land, to a land*
> *flowing with milk and honey, to the place of the*
> *Canaanites and the Hittites and the Amorites and*
> *the Perizzites and the Hivites and the Jebusites.*
> *Now therefore, behold, the cry of the children*
> *of Israel has come to Me, and I have also seen*
> *the oppression with which the Egyptians oppress*
> *them. Come now, therefore, and I will send you*
> *to Pharaoh that you may bring My people,*
> *the children of Israel, out of Egypt."*
> (Ex. 3:7–10)

God has not been asleep, on vacation, or indifferent to the slavery and sorrows of His people. He's been watching for 400 years. We might be tempted to ask, "Why did God wait so long to decide to deliver His people from their oppressor?" Have you ever asked Him that question for yourself? "God, how long before you deliver me from this thing?" Whatever it is—a difficult boss, financial hardship, anxiety, worry, depression. I would suggest that there are some things that God does in a progressive way.

> *"Behold, I send an Angel before you to keep you in the way and to bring you into the place which I have prepared. Beware of Him and obey His voice; do not provoke Him, for He will not pardon your transgressions; for My name is in Him. But if you indeed obey His voice and do all that I speak, then I will be an enemy to your enemies and an adversary to your adversaries. For My Angel will go before you and bring you in to the Amorites and the Hittites and the Perizzites and the Canaanites and the Hivites and the Jebusites; and I will cut them off."*
> (Ex. 23:20–23)

Later in the same chapter, we read:

> *"I will not drive them out from before you in one year, lest the land become desolate and the beasts of the field become too numerous for you. Little by*

little I will drive them out from before you, until
you have increased, and you inherit the land. And
I will set your bounds from the Red Sea to the sea,
Philistia, and from the desert to the River. For I
will deliver the inhabitants of the land into your
hand, and you shall drive them out before you."
(vv. 29–31)

God has prepared a place for His people and sent His Angel (note that Angel is spelled with a capital *A* in the New King James Version, suggesting the pre-incarnate Jesus) to go before them to bring them into the place prepared for them. Here is the Mediator at work long before His physical appearance upon the earth. However, they must learn to obey His voice and do what He says. This is their preparation for the place prepared for them. Notice that He is going to drive them out little by little until they have increased enough to inherit the land. Otherwise, the beasts of the field will become too numerous for them, and they would lose what they've gained.

What does God mean when He says the land would become desolate and the beasts of the field would become overwhelming if He drove their enemies out in a short time? Our land—our internal spiritual land—must not be desolate. It must be built up and filled with faith, trust, courage, and authority. This does not happen overnight.

I can't just put on the uniform and go out on the field. There must be preparation for the challenges that are going to come. That preparation takes place on the practice field, not on the playing field.

The Israelites have been on the practice field for 400 years under the cruel and rigorous treatment of Pharaoh and his taskmasters. God has decided it is now time for them to get into the game. He has handpicked a mediator, Moses, to negotiate the terms of their release. He says to Moses in Exodus 3:10, "Come now, therefore, and I will send you to Pharaoh that you may bring My people, the children of Israel, out of Egypt." He is about to lead his people out of bondage. Whatever or whoever has us bound, God is bound and determined by His love to release us and bring us out!

God tells Moses in Exodus 3:17 to tell the people that He's going to bring them out of the affliction of Egypt to a land flowing with milk and honey. Psalm 34:19 says, "Many are the afflictions of the righteous, but the LORD delivers them out of them all."

How do I know this is true? First, the Bible tells me so, and I choose to believe it. However, I also have the experience of affliction, and He has delivered me out of it. I can now bear witness to the truth of His word. I have seen Him do it. I can give eyewitness testimony to it.

Furthermore, God is not only going to bring them out; He's going to bring them in to a land flowing with milk and honey. What is the significance of milk and honey? It reminds me of a baby crying, and the mother takes that baby up into her arms and feeds it with warm milk so that the baby is quieted and at peace. The honey brings to mind the sweetness of the presence of the Lord and the fullness of joy in His presence. Isaiah 55:12 says, "For you shall go out with joy, and be led out with peace."

After God tells Moses that He's going to bring His people out from under the strong hand of Pharaoh, He lets him know that it's not going to be easy. God says to him in Exodus 3:19, "I am sure that the king of Egypt will not let you go, no, not even by a mighty hand." We have an adversary, the devil, who does not want to let us go, who "walks about like a roaring lion, seeking whom he may devour" (1 Peter 5:8) He does not give up his efforts to steal, kill, and destroy the life of Christ within us. In Luke 22:31–32a, the Lord Jesus informs Peter that Satan has asked permission to sift him as wheat. But the Lord Jesus goes on to tell Peter that He has prayed for him that his faith in the Lord Jesus would not fail. It may falter, but Jesus prayed that in the end it will not fail.

There are two things to take note of here. First, the enemy of our soul can only do to us what God permits him to do. He is not free to do whatever he wants. Second, whatever God permits the enemy to do is for God's purpose, not for the enemy's purpose. God uses our enemy as an instrument for **our** benefit, not **his**.

It is God's intent to produce in us an unfailing faith in Him that becomes more and more established with every permitted assault of the enemy. 1 Peter 5:10 says, "May the God of all grace, who called us to His eternal glory by Christ Jesus, after you have suffered a while, perfect, establish, strengthen, and settle you." And that settles it!

Back to Exodus—God goes on to tell Moses in Exodus 3:20 that He's going to stretch out His hand and strike Egypt with all of His wonders which He will do in their midst, and when He's done, the king of Egypt **will** let you go. Furthermore, He tells Moses that when you go, you will **not** go empty-handed.

What we see here is that we have a Mediator who not only negotiates our release from our captor, but he takes an active role in securing our release. In 2 Chronicles 20, Jehoshaphat, the king of Judah, was informed that a conglomerate of armies had been formed to do battle against him, which scared him to the point that he proclaimed a fast throughout all of Judah to seek the Lord. During the fast, the spirit of the Lord came upon Jahaziel in the midst of the assembly. He prophesied to king Jehoshaphat that he should not be afraid because of this great multitude coming against him. Why? Because the battle is not yours to fight. The Lord your God is going to fight it. We need to know that when we're faced with overwhelming odds and greatly outmatched, it's time for God to shine and display His unequaled and unrivaled majestic power on behalf of all those who put their trust in Him.

We also need to know that we're not going to come out of it empty-handed, not so much in a physical sense, but spiritually. Our trust in our Mediator, who fights for us, is going to be fortified to a higher level. If we're willing, each battle increases the strength of our faith and trust in our God, if we don't give into the temptation to faint and lose heart. Help us, Lord! Lead us **not** into that temptation!

Now Moses had the word and directive of the Lord, the Great I Am, who appeared to him in the burning bush. However, he posed the question to the Lord, "What if they don't believe me? What if they don't believe that You sent me?" The issue here is authority. Pharaoh essentially says to Moses, "By whose authority do you come here to challenge our authority?" We must remember that Egypt was the ruling authority in the world at that time, and then Moses came on behalf of the enslaved Israelites, demanding that he set them free. And not only that, but also demanding that the Egyptians shower them with articles of silver, gold, and clothing. Pharoah's response would likely be, "Are you kidding me? Who do you think you are?"

The gracious Great I Am did not chide or rebuke Moses for questioning whether the Egyptians would believe him. He gave Moses a demonstration of His authority, turning Moses's rod into a snake and back into a rod again, "That they may believe that the LORD... has appeared to you" (Ex. 4:5). The Lord God then gave Moses another sign, turning his hand leprous and then restoring it back to normal.

This is a foreshadowing of our Mediator, the Lord Jesus, who said in John 4:48, "Unless you people see signs and wonders, you will by no means believe." Nicodemus, a ruler of the Jews, came to Jesus secretly by night and said to Jesus that no one could do the signs that Jesus was doing unless God was with him. Declaration must be confirmed by demonstration. Talk is cheap unless there is action to validate it.

God spoke further to Moses in Exodus 4:9, telling him that if the Egyptians don't believe the two signs He's given him, he should take water from the river and pour it out on the dry land, and it will turn into blood. And so, God convinced Moses that he was His man, His mediator, to negotiate the release of His people from their slavery to the Egyptians by means of mighty signs and wonders.

Moses and Aaron went to Egypt and spoke to Pharaoh by the word of the Lord, commanding him to let His people go. However, Pharaoh was not so inclined to release the people of God, as he stated in Exodus 5:2, "Who is the LORD, that I should obey His voice…? I do not know the LORD, nor will I let Israel go." However, Pharaoh was about to find out who the Lord was, as the Lord said to Moses in Exodus 6:1, "Now you shall see what I will do to Pharaoh. For with a strong hand he will let them go, and with a strong hand he will drive them out of his land."

God then reminded Moses that He was the Lord, Yahweh, the covenant-keeping God. God went on speaking to Moses in Exodus 6:3–8:

> *I appeared to Abraham, to Isaac, and to Jacob, as God Almighty, but by My name LORD I was not known to them. I have also established My covenant with them, to give them the land of Canaan, the land of their pilgrimage, in which they were strangers. And I have also heard the groaning of the children of Israel whom*

the Egyptians keep in bondage, and I have remembered My covenant. Therefore say to the children of Israel: 'I am the LORD; I will bring you out from under the burdens of the Egyptians, I will rescue you from their bondage, and I will redeem you with an outstretched arm and with great judgments. I will take you as My people, and I will be your God. Then you shall know that I am the LORD your God who brings you out from under the burdens of the Egyptians. And I will bring you into the land which I swore to give to Abraham, Isaac, and Jacob; and I will give it to you as a heritage: I am the LORD.'"

Yahweh is a covenant-keeping God. He delivers on His promises. He keeps His word sooner or later. I like the sooner; I'm not crazy about the later. However, I am learning that God has a purpose in the later. It is a test of our faith in Him. Am I going to continue to trust Him? Am I going to continue to wait on Him? The more we continue to trust and wait, the greater and stronger our faith in Him becomes, and that is the point of it all! Psalm 27:14 says, "Wait on the LORD; be of good courage, and He shall strengthen your heart; wait, I say, on the LORD!"

In Exodus 7:5, God says to Moses, "The Egyptians shall know that I am the LORD, when I stretch out My hand on Egypt and bring out the children of Israel from among them." This reminds me of Psalm 46:10, which is often quoted as speaking to us, "Be still, and know that I am God." However, when we look at the overall content of this psalm, it could very well be speaking to our enemies about coming to our aid. "Be still. **I** am their God, not **you!**" God is determined to prove to our enemies (and to us) that **He** is the Lord. However, we are the proving ground. Job was the proving ground for God to prove to Satan that He is God and that Job was His man, come hell or high water.

The release of the Israelites would begin, and that is important to know. It was the beginning of a gradual release over a period of time, marked by a series of events. As we noted earlier, our adversary, the devil, is reluctant and resistant to letting us alone and letting us go. However, our Advocate and Mediator, the Lord Jesus, has already negotiated our release through his death on the cross, assuring us that the God of Peace shall soon crush Satan under our feet (Romans 16:20). How soon, we don't know. All we know is that sooner or later it shall be so because His word is true and He cannot lie.

God began the release by commanding Aaron to throw down his rod before Pharaoh, and when he did, it turned into a serpent (Ex.7:10). However, Pharaoh called his magicians, and they were able to do the same (Ex. 7:11). Even so, Aaron's rod swallowed up all their rods (Ex. 7:12). However, Pharaoh was not impressed. He hardened his heart, refusing to let them go (Ex.7:13).

The God of Israel was just getting started. He's warming up. That's why we should never give up. He then commanded

Moses to take his rod and strike the waters which are in the river, their primary source of water, and they would be turned into blood. The fish would die, the river would stink, and the Egyptians would not be able to drink the water. And not only the river, but every source of water—the streams, the ponds, and all their pools of water. Even the water they have in buckets and pitchers (Ex. 7:17–19).

However, once again, the magicians of Egypt were able to duplicate this sign. Once again, Pharaoh's heart was hardened. Once again, he refused to let the people go. Again, this represents the battle we go through as believers to be released from the lust of our flesh and past sinful behaviors. The sins of generations passed on to us: fear, worry, anxiety, depression. These were rooted in us before coming to Christ. Remember, He receives us just as we are, as stated in the old hymn "Just as I Am," which was sung at the close of each Billy Graham Crusade. Stanza three is especially applicable to this subject:

> *Just as I am, though tossed about*
> *With many a conflict, many a doubt,*
> *Fightings and fears within, without,*
> *O Lamb of God, I come, I come.*[23]

Moving on, we see that God continues sending plagues on Egypt.

> *And the LORD spoke to Moses, "Go to Pharaoh*
> *and say to him, 'Thus says the LORD: "Let My*

---

[23] Charlotte Elliott, *"Just As I Am,"* 1835, public domain.

*people go, that they may serve Me. But if you
refuse to let them go, behold, I will smite all
your territory with frogs. So the river shall
bring forth frogs abundantly, which shall go up
and come into your house, into your bedroom,
on your bed, into the houses of your servants,
on your people, into your ovens, and into your
kneading bowls. And the frogs shall come
up on you, on your people, and on all your
servants.* " ' "
(Ex. 8:1–4)

Frogs everywhere, can you imagine that? In your bed
when you're trying to sleep, in your bowls and pans when
you're trying to prepare your food. In your ovens when
you're cooking your food. Everywhere you go in your house,
there are frogs. In the living room, dining room, kitchen,
bathroom, in the shower. You can't get away from them.
Frogs are unclean creatures in the Bible. They also represent
unclean spirits—lustful, shameful, proud, rebellious spirits.
Have you ever been plagued with unclean thoughts that you
just couldn't get rid of?

In Exodus 8:8, Pharaoh couldn't stand it anymore and
called for Moses to call upon the Lord to take away the frogs
from him and his people. He promised he would let the
children of Israel go. What is interesting to note here is that
Pharaoh's magicians also brought up frogs on the land of
Egypt with their enchantments, or "secret arts." However,

Pharaoh did not call upon them to remove them. He asked Moses to call upon God to remove them. The magicians could bring them, but they couldn't remove them.

This is much like our adversary who brings affliction upon us but can't remove it because he won't remove it. But the Bible says, "Many are the afflictions of the righteous, but the Lord delivers him out of them all" (Psalm 34:19).

And so, Moses cried out to the Lord concerning the frogs which He had brought against Pharaoh, and the Lord listened to Moses, and the frogs all died—every one of them, everywhere they were. And in like manner, when we cry out to the Lord, He answers. Isaiah 30:19b says, "[The Lord] will be very gracious to you at the sound of your cry; when He hears it, He will answer you."

Pharaoh said he would let the people go if Moses would entreat the Lord to take away the frogs. That word *entreat* means to plead with or beg the Lord to take away the frogs.[24]

I don't know how often we, as Christians, have considered pleading with or begging God for a thing. Perhaps we feel it's beneath us as "King's Kids." However, I would draw our attention to the word *kids*. We are children of God, which means that there will be times when a certain thing is way too big for us, way too strong for us, and as children, we desperately cry out, plead, even beg for our Father's intervention. In fact, in those situations, He is waiting to

---

[24] Jack W. Hayford et al., *New Spirit-Filled Life Bible: New International Version* (Nashville: Thomas Nelson, 2015).

hear this. We can fight, and we can have faith, but it will not avail much if God is waiting for our cry.

Pharaoh said he would let the people go, but once the frogs were gone, he hardened his heart and refused to let them go. How many people have we known that have had what we might call "jailhouse conversions"? They pray, "God, if you get me out of this, I'll serve You forever." God gets them out of whatever the situation was, and when the heat is off, they forget what they said to God and go back to their old ways. They were just using God for their own purposes, and when He had answered their prayer, they no longer had any use for God. Our God does not want to be used for our purposes; He wants to use us for His purposes. He desires a relationship with us in which we have the same love for Him that He has for us. He was willing to sacrifice his only begotten Son—all that He had. He wants us to love Him for Him alone with all that we have, with all of our heart, mind, soul, and strength.

Despite Pharaoh's resistance, God was by no means finished with him. This time, He turned all the dust of the land of Egypt into lice or gnats. And this time, Pharaoh's magicians were not able to duplicate this sign as they did with the others, leading them to conclude that this was, indeed, "the finger of God" (Ex. 8:19). Lice or gnats were all over the Egyptians and their animals, but still, Pharaoh's heart hardened, and he would not let the people go.

However, Pharaoh would discover that he was no match for the God of Israel. God would also make a distinction between His people, who lived in Goshen, and the Egyptians. He sent swarms of flies into Egypt, but not into Goshen, where His people lived. All the livestock of Egypt were struck with disease and died, but not the livestock of His people. Boils came upon the Egyptians and their animals, but not on the Israelites and their animals. Hail, like Egypt had never seen since its founding, rained down upon and destroyed every man and animal in Egypt that was not sheltered, but there was no hail in Goshen.

Swarms of locusts covered the ground in Egypt so that the ground was no longer visible. The locusts ate the best of the vegetation in Egypt that the hail had left. They filled their houses and the houses of their servants and all the houses of the Egyptians. But they did not cover the ground or fill the houses of the Israelites in Goshen.

Darkness came upon the land of Egypt for three days—a deep, foreboding, depressing darkness that could be felt. So much so, that the Egyptians did not see one another or go out from their houses for three days. This is an apt description of the outer darkness of hell, which will last a lot longer than three days for those who refuse to receive the Mediator, the Lord Jesus, as their Deliverer and Savior. There was no such oppressive darkness in Goshen. The children of Israel had light in their dwellings.

Finally, God told Moses that He would bring one more plague on Pharaoh and on Egypt, and this time Pharaoh would let the children of Israel go. This time, all the firstborn in the land of Egypt would die, from the firstborn of Pharaoh to the firstborn of the female servants and the firstborn of the animals.

What is the significance of the plague upon the firstborn? In Genesis 49:3, Jacob refers to his firstborn son, Reuben, as the first sign of his strength, excelling in honor, excelling in power. In the book of Numbers chapter 3:13, it says that every firstborn of Israel belongs to God. Deuteronomy 21:17 states that a double portion of all that a father has shall be given to the firstborn son, "for he is the beginning of his strength, the right of the first born is his."

We see by this that God would strike and cut off the first sign of the Egyptians' strength, their prized possession, and when He does, they **will** let the Israelites go. The release will finally come, having been mediated by God's man, Moses.

However, the final release came against all odds when God hardened Pharaoh's heart, at which point Pharaoh, once again, changed his mind and decided to go after the Israelites. He overtook them at the Red Sea. Why would God harden Pharaoh's heart and allow him to go after His people after He finally convinced Pharaoh to let them go? Have you ever wondered that in your own life? God has set you free in some way from the adversary, only to find that he is pursuing you once again, and trying to take you out? However, as we shall see, the adversary is not going to succeed in taking us out.

The Israelites were trapped between the oncoming army of Pharaoh in front of them and the Red Sea behind them, a most impossible situation. Why would God do this? Moses said to the people in Exodus 14:13, "Do not be afraid. Stand still, and see the salvation of the Lord, which *He* will accomplish for you today. For the Egyptians whom you see today, you shall see again no more forever" (emphasis added).

God parted the Red Sea with an unprecedented east wind, allowing His people to go right through on dry land to the other side. However, when the Egyptians pursued them, God called off the wind. When the Egyptians were smack dab in the middle of it, the Red Sea came crashing down upon Pharaoh and everyone with him, drowning them all. So, why did God harden Pharaoh's heart to go after His people? To bring him out in order to take him out!

There is a day coming when our adversary, the enemy of our soul, is going to be brought out of the bottomless pit one final time at the end of time as we know it.

> *"He who has an ear, let him hear what the Spirit says to the churches. To him who overcomes I will give to eat from the tree of life, which is in the midst of the Paradise of God...*

> *"These things says the First and the Last, who was dead, and came to life: 'I know your works, tribulation, and poverty (but you are rich); and I know the blasphemy of those who say they are Jews and are not, but are a synagogue of Satan. Do not fear any of those things which you are*

*about to suffer. Indeed, the devil is about to throw
some of you into prison, that you may be tested,
and you will have tribulation ten days. Be faithful
until death, and I will give you the crown of life.'"*
(Rev. 2:7–10)

And so shall the release be finalized, forever!

Chapter Five

The Result

Years after he fulfilled his God-given mandate to release the children of Israel from slavery to the Egyptians, Moses died. What would happen to the Israelites now? What was to be the result of their release?

> *After the death of Moses the servant of the Lord,*
> *it came to pass that the LORD spoke to Joshua the*
> *son of Nun, Moses' assistant, saying: "Moses*
> *My servant is dead. Now therefore, arise, go*
> *over this Jordan, you and all this people, to the*
> *land which I am giving to them—the children of*
> *Israel. Every place that the sole of your foot will*
> *tread upon I have given you, as I said to Moses.*
> *From the wilderness and this Lebanon as far as*
> *the great river, the River Euphrates, all the land*
> *of the Hittites, and to the Great Sea toward the*
> *going down of the sun, shall be your territory. No*
> *man shall be able to stand before you all the days*

of your life; as I was with Moses, so I will be with
you. I will not leave you nor forsake you. Be strong
and of good courage, for to this people you shall
divide as an inheritance the land which I swore to
their fathers to give them. Only be strong and very
courageous, that you may observe to do according
to all the law which Moses My servant commanded
you; do not turn from it to the right hand or to the
left, that you may prosper wherever you go. This
Book of the Law shall not depart from your mouth,
but you shall meditate in it day and night, that you
may observe to do according to all that is written
in it. For then you will make your way prosperous,
and then you will have good success. Have I not
commanded you? Be strong and of good courage;
do not be afraid, nor be dismayed, for the Lord
your God is with you wherever you go."
(Josh. 1:1–9)

God now turns his attention to Joshua, Moses's protégé. He speaks to him as He has spoken to Moses. "The Lord spoke to Moses face to face, as a man speaks to his friend" (Ex. 33:11a). First of all, it is important to take note of where Moses was when God spoke to him. He was in the tabernacle, which was constructed under the supervision of Moses to be the dwelling place of the Lord, a place set apart to meet with the Lord. It is so important that we have a meeting place where we get alone with the Lord, talk to Him, and listen to Him. In Matthew 6:6, the Lord Jesus told us that when we pray we are to go into our room, shut out everything and everyone else, and get alone with God, "who is in the secret place." You can't hear God in the public place with all the noise and hustle and bustle. He's in the secret place, waiting for us to come in where it's quiet and get alone with Him.

This is the place where God spoke to Moses. I have experienced in my life that this is the place where God speaks to us—in the quiet of the secret place. Joshua, Moses's servant, learned this from Moses and "did not depart from the tabernacle" (Ex. 33:11b). And so, God now spoke with Joshua as He had spoken with Moses.

We see an example of this same truth in the life of the prophet Elijah in 1 Kings 19. God worked mightily through him to execute the prophets of the pagan god Baal, whom Jezebel, the wife of King Ahab, brought into the house of Israel. She became infuriated with Elijah and vowed to kill him, causing him to run for his life out into the wilderness. He was so distraught that he asked the Lord to take his life. God told him to "go out, and stand on the mountain before the LORD" (1 Kings 19:11). When he did, a great wind attacked the mountains, but the Lord was not in the wind. After the wind, came an earthquake, but the Lord was not in the earthquake. After the earthquake, there was a fire. But the Lord was not in the fire. After the fire, Elijah heard a still small voice—the voice of the Lord. Elijah heard the Lord's voice in the quietness, not in the noise of the wind, the earthquake, or the crackling of the fire.

Joshua was in the right place at the right time to hear the voice of the Lord. And what did he hear? That he was to be the successor to his mentor, Moses. He picked up where Moses left off and brought the children of Israel into the Promised Land that God was giving them.

If we are ever going to know what God requires of us, what His will and purposes are for us, we are going to have to be diligent to continually get into the quiet of the secret place with Him.

When Jesus's disciples asked him to teach them to pray, part of His teaching to them was to ask their Father in heaven to give them this day, their daily bread. I would suggest that the Lord Jesus was not just talking about Rye bread, but more so, the bread of the word and will of God. In fact, Jesus refers to Himself in John 6:51 as "the living bread which came down from heaven. If anyone eats of this bread, he will live forever." What is the bread of which He speaks? I believe it is the words He speaks as well as taking in, taking to heart, and believing what He speaks. Believing that He is the Way, the Truth, and the Life, and that no one comes to the Father but through Him.

It is believing that His death on the cross was the payment for our sin. Believing that in Him we have eternal life. Believing that by faith in Him, we are in right standing with God and have peace with God. John 1:1 says, "In the beginning was the Word, and the Word was with God, and the Word was God." John 1:14 clarifies this further by stating that "the Word became flesh and dwelt among us." This is speaking of Jesus, the Son of God, the Word of God.

Joshua heard the voice of the Lord as he was faithful to "tabernacle" with the Lord in the secret place. Not only was he given the charge to lead the children of Israel into the land He had promised them, but God gave him explicit details regarding all that he was giving them along the way. Wherever they walked along the way belonged to them. The wilderness, Lebanon, the river Euphrates, and all the land of the Hittites and into the Great Sea would be their territory. (Josh. 1:3–4)

This is so much like our journey with the Lord in our own lives. As we are faithful to spend time alone with the Lord in the secret place, we will hear Him speaking to us, directing us in the way we should go. He gives us the assurance that if we go, He has already given it to us. It will succeed!

God goes on to assure Joshua in verse five that "No man shall be able to stand before you all the days of your life; as I was with Moses, so I will be with you. I will not leave you nor forsake you."

We have the same promise in our journey with the Lord. Jesus, who said to His disciples before He ascended into heaven with the Father, "I am with you always, even to the end of the age" (Matthew 28:20). The "end of the age" means the end of this life and forever. Because of His presence with us, no opposition will prevail against us. Romans 8:31 says, "If God is for us, who can be against us?" Since there are those who would set themselves against us, I submit that Paul in writing this was saying,

"Who can be against us *and prevail*?" No one! Isaiah 54:17 says, "No weapon formed against you shall prosper." That word *prosper* in the Hebrew means "to advance, to make progress, or to succeed."[25] A weapon may come against us and cause us consternation, but it will not succeed in its evil intent to take us down and take us out. God will simply not allow it. It will have to retreat and withdraw, and we will go on our way. I like to say, "it may assail, but it shall not prevail."

Another lesson we can learn from Joshua and the children of Israel is not only the taking of outward territory, but the taking of inward territory. Many of us harbor territories of anxiety, worry, fear, doubt, or depression. These territories must be taken and overcome, which God has already promised to do for us.

The Lord Jesus said, in John 14:27, "Peace I leave with you, My peace I give to you…Let not your heart be troubled, neither let it be afraid." In Matthew chapter six, the Lord Jesus also tells us not to worry about our life. If our Heavenly Father can feed the birds, He can certainly take care of us. Jesus makes it clear that worry accomplishes nothing. It is a useless activity. Faith in God accomplishes infinitely more. Psalm 16:11 says that in the presence of the Lord, there is fullness of joy. There is no depression in His presence. There is no fear in His love.

---

[25] Jack W. Hayford et al., *New Spirit-Filled Life Bible: New International Version* (Nashville: Thomas Nelson, 2015).

God further said to Joshua, in verse six of this first chapter of the book of Joshua, to be strong and of good courage. I have discovered that God does not command us to do something unless He's committed to making it happen. What He commands, He commissions. I like to say that we do the believing of it, and God does the working of it.

He is commanding Joshua to be strong and of good courage. It takes courage to be willing to take on something bigger and stronger than you, something greater than your capability. Again, this is where our faith in God comes into play. We have got to believe that although it may be bigger or stronger than us, it is not even close to being bigger or stronger than our God. Ephesians 6:10 commands us to "be strong in the Lord and in the power of His might." Psalm 121:1–2 says in part, "Where does my help come from? My help comes from the LORD" (NIV).

God encouraged Joshua a second time in verse seven, after charging him with the task of conquering and taking the land God swore to give to their ancestors. This time He said, "Only be strong, and very courageous." Not just courageous, but **very courageous**.

The Hebrew word for strong is *chazaq* (khaw-zak›).[26] It means to be valiant, strengthened, firm, fortified, established. God is not telling Joshua that he must have the strength to accomplish the task. He's telling him to have the strength of

---

[26] Strong, James. "1288 חָזַק (*khaw-zak'*)," Strong's Hebrew: 1288. חָזַק (*khaw-zak'*) (Strong's Concordance, 2025), https://strongsconcordance.org/

resolve to just go. When he goes, God will be with him in it, and God will give him success in it.

The Hebrew word for courageous is *amats* (aw-mats').[27] It also means to be strong, but adds the meaning of brave, bold, determined, and decisive. In other words, to make up your mind to do a thing. James 1:8 says that a double-minded person is unstable in all their ways. You can't count on them. They might say yes today, but they are nowhere to be found tomorrow. God is looking for those who have the courage to stick with it, believing God for it.

God went on to say to Joshua in verse seven, "That you may observe to do according to all the law which Moses My servant commanded you; do not turn from it to the right hand or to the left." Whatever he told you to do, do it! Don't think you can take matters into your own hands and do it your own way. Proverbs 14:12 says that there is a way that seems right to our human way of thinking, but in the end it leads to death. Isaiah 55:9 says that the way God thinks is higher than the way we think. God sees the whole picture from beginning to end, because He is the Beginning and the End. Our vision is limited by our finite existence. We don't know what tomorrow may bring; God does.

God further elaborated this point to Joshua in verse eight, stating in essence that he shall continually have the

---

[27] Strong, James. "553 אָמֵץ (*aw-mats'*)," Strong's Hebrew: 553. אָמֵץ (*aw-mats'*) (Strong's Concordance, 2025), https://strongsconcordance.org/

word of God in his mouth. He shall meditate on it day and night.

The Hebrew word for meditate is *hagah* (daw-gaw')[28] which means to reflect upon, to repeat and allow to sink into a firm hold or understanding.[29] God's word is my compass; it is what I go by, how I think and make decisions. Proverbs 3:5–6 says that we should not lean on, or depend on, our own understanding, but that in all our ways we should acknowledge Him. The word *acknowledge* means to know in the sense of finding out.[30] I need to find out what way God has for me before I choose the way to go. How often do we do that? Speaking for myself, I would say "not often enough."

In verse nine, God again commanded Joshua to be strong and of good courage. However, this time He added to it that Joshua should not be afraid or dismayed. The Hebrew word for afraid is *arats* (aw-rats').[31] It is a very strong word. It means to be very afraid, in fact, to tremble and be terrified. Have you ever been so afraid of something you had to do or someone you had to face that you were terrified?

[28] Strong, James. "1897 הָגָה (*daw-gaw'*)," Strong's Hebrew: 1897. הָגָה (*daw-gaw'*) (Strong's Concordance, 2025), https://strongsconcordance.org/

[29] Jack W. Hayford et al., *New Spirit-Filled Life Bible: New International Version* (Nashville: Thomas Nelson, 2015).

[30] Jack W. Hayford et al., *New Spirit-Filled Life Bible: New International Version* (Nashville: Thomas Nelson, 2015).

[31] Strong, James. "6206 עָרַץ ` (*aw-rats'*)," Strong's Hebrew: 6206. עָרַץ ` (*aw-rats'*) (Strong's Concordance, 2025), https://strongsconcordance.org/

God goes on to tell Joshua that neither should he be dismayed. The Hebrew word for dismayed is *chathath* (khaw-thath›).[32] It means to be scared to the point of being shattered and broken.

Let's face it, there are some things that God allows in our lives that are way bigger and stronger than we are. The task that God was charging Joshua with was bigger than he was. If we're ever going to know how big and how great is our God, to whom we sing praises, we're going to have to be put into situations bigger and stronger than we are to prove it. I'm not crazy about being put in those situations, but I'm absolutely thrilled when He shows up and shows Himself strong in a way that I never could. God is determined to make believers out of us, and so we should not be surprised when we find ourselves in situations too big for us. They are only meant to strengthen and fortify our faith in our God.

*Beloved, do not think it strange concerning
the fiery trial which is to try you, as though
some strange thing happened to you; but rejoice
to the extent that you partake of Christ's
sufferings, that when His glory is revealed,
you may also be glad with exceeding joy.*
(1 Peter 4:12-13)

---

[32] Strong, James. "2865 חָתַת (*khaw-thath'*)," Strong's Hebrew: 2865. חָתַת (*khaw-thath'*) (Strong's Concordance, 2025), https://strongsconcordance.org/

God then lets Joshua know why he should not be terrified, shattered, or broken, "For the LORD your God is with you wherever you go" (Josh. 1:9). God wasn't just sending Joshua, He was going with him. This was God's plan, and He needed a man to join with Him to fulfill it. They were in this together. Joshua was not going to work for God, he was going to work with God to bring the Israelites into the Promised Land. The same is true for all of us who belong to God. We work with Him, and He with us, to fulfill His plan for us. I am not an employee; I am a shareholder. I get to share in what is His. And more than that, I am a son, a daughter, an heir (Rom. 8:16-17). The word *heir* means to possess with another.[33] It is a joint sharing in that which belongs to another. We are joint heirs with Christ of all that the Father has given to Him.

This is similar to children being heirs of their parents. They become the beneficiaries of what their parents worked for because they are their children. They were born to them and have their DNA inside them. Jesus said in John 3:7 that we must be born again, born of the Spirit of God. When we were born the first time, we became the children of our parents. When we were born the second time, born of the Spirit, we became the children of God, and therefore, heirs of God.

Once again, an heir is the recipient of that for which they did not work. This is grace—receiving the benefit of that for

---

[33] Jack W. Hayford et al., *New Spirit-Filled Life Bible: New International Version* (Nashville: Thomas Nelson, 2015).

which I did not work. Someone else worked for it and gave it to me. Ephesians 2:8–9 says, "For by grace you have been saved through faith, and that not of yourselves; it is the gift of God, not of works, lest anyone should boast." Jesus lived a sinless life upon the earth, and then gave that spotless, sinless life to us. He worked by dying on the cross, paying the penalty for our sin and gifting to us eternal life, saving us from eternal death. That is pure grace, and that is what we live on. Not anything we worked for, but everything He worked for, for us. We will spend the rest of eternity thanking Him for it. Thanking Him for saving us from the never-ending torture of a never-ending hell, forever separated, isolated from God and all our loved ones. Thank you, thank you, Lord Jesus!

Joshua has been fully encouraged and strengthened by the Lord. Joshua 1:10–11 says that Joshua commanded the officers, "Pass through the camp and command the people, saying, 'Prepare provisions for yourselves, for within three days you will cross over this Jordan, to go in to possess the land which the LORD your God is giving you to possess.'" Verse 16 lets us know that he receives a favorable response from the people, "All that you command us we will do, and wherever you send us we will go."

And so, the journey to the Promised Land began. The journey was not without obstacles, without opposition, or without battles, just as our journey with the Lord into the land He's promised us is not without the same. However, the difference for us is that the land God has promised us is not a physical land, but a spiritual land. Spiritual well-being that includes peace, joy, and the love of God filling our hearts and souls. Romans 14:17 says that the Kingdom of God is not a matter of eating and drinking and the possession of things of this world, but of righteousness, peace, and joy by the power of the Holy Spirit.

Joshua and the Israelites traveled through Jericho on their way to the Promised Land. However, before they got to Jericho, they had to cross the Jordan River, which at this time was at flood stage. Crossing it would have been life-threatening, with the potential to drown the thousands of Israelites. How would they ever be able to cross the Jordan?

So it was, when the people set out from their camp to cross over the Jordan, with the priests bearing the ark of the covenant before the people, and as those who bore the ark came to the Jordan, and the feet of the priests who bore the ark dipped in the edge of the water (for the Jordan overflows all its banks during the whole time of harvest), that the waters which came down from upstream stood still, and rose in a heap very far away at Adam, the city that is beside Zaretan. So the waters that went down into the Sea of the Arabah, the Salt Sea, failed, and were cut off; and the people crossed over opposite Jericho. Then the priests who bore the ark of the covenant of the Lord stood firm on dry ground in the

*midst of the Jordan; and all Israel crossed over
on dry ground, until all the people had crossed
completely over the Jordan.*
(Josh. 3:14–17)

The priests, the spiritual leaders of the Israelites, bore the Ark of the Covenant. Why? It symbolized God's promise of His presence with them wherever He told them to go. As long as they recognized and honored His presence with them, nothing would keep them from entering the land God had promised to them.

God told Joshua and the priests and the people to cross over the Jordan. They didn't have boats. They didn't have any way to cross aside from their legs and feet. What they did have were spiritual leaders, bearing the ark of God's presence and willing to step into the waters of the Jordan River. And as soon as they did, the water stood still and rose up in a heap like the Red Sea had when Moses lifted up his staff at the command of the Lord.

The priests stood firm on dry ground in the middle of the Jordan until all the people had crossed completely over the river. All Israel crossed over on dry ground!

Have you ever been confronted by a situation that was far greater than you, far greater than your physical, mental, and emotional ability? You didn't have a boat. However, like the Israelites, you have the promise of His presence with you. And this is where faith comes in. Am I willing to believe God and that His presence is with me? Am I willing to step into the water? Am I willing to step into whatever situation I'm facing? This is what true faith is. It's more than something I say. It is something I do, and it is confirmed by the action I take and opens the way for God to step in. There is no way around it. There is no other way to truly know that God is with me than to take that first step. James 2:26 says that faith without works, without action, is dead. It does not make way for God to step in and breathe His life into it.

Isaiah 43:1–2 says:

> *But now, thus says the LORD, who created you,*
> *O Jacob,*
> *And He who formed you, O Israel:*
> *"Fear not, for I have redeemed you;*
> *I have called you by your name;*
> *You are Mine.*
> *When you pass through the waters, I will be with you;*
> *And through the rivers, they shall not overflow you.*
> *When you walk through the fire, you shall not be*
> *burned,*
> *Nor shall the flame scorch you."*

This is the promise we have, but we must be willing to step into the fire or the water and keep going until we lay hold of the promise. Notice that it says, "when you pass through the waters," and "when you walk through the fire."

How many of us have had to pass through some things that threatened to drown us, burn us, and consume us? There are some trials that God does not keep us from, but He promises to keep us in the midst of them. They will not drown us, they will not scorch us, they will not consume us. In fact, what they will do is make our faith in our faithful God that much stronger, confirming that the God we say we believe in is truly the God we do believe in. That is exactly God's purpose in it. He is determined to prove to us that we can trust Him, come hell or high water. And like his servant Job, He is determined to prove that we are truly His. Personally, I wish it could come some other way, some easier way, but if that's the way it comes, then Holy Spirit help me to step into it, trusting You to take me through it.

All of the Israelites had completely crossed over the Jordan on their way to the Promised Land. This was just the first sign of God's presence and promise to get them there. All they have to do is keep believing Him, keep proving it, and keep going. Our adversary, the devil, is determined to stop us from going forward in our journey with the Lord. However, we have an Advocate who is more determined to get us there and frustrate every attempt of our adversary to stop us.

Once the people had completely crossed over the Jordan River on dry ground, God spoke to Joshua to take twelve men from the people, one from every tribe. Each man was to take a stone out of the river—twelve stones in all. They were then instructed to set the twelve stones up on the other side of the river as memorial stones in Gilgal. Then God had Joshua speak to the people regarding the purpose for it.

Then he spoke to the children of Israel, saying:
"When your children ask their fathers in time
to come, saying, 'What are these stones?'
then you shall let your children know, saying,
'Israel crossed over this Jordan on dry land';
for the LORD your God dried up the waters of the
Jordan before you until you had crossed over,
as the LORD your God did to the Red Sea, which
He dried up before us until we had crossed over,
that all the peoples of the earth may know the
hand of the LORD, that it is mighty, that you may
fear the LORD your God forever."
(Josh. 4:21–24)

It is paramount that we always remember God's faithfulness in the past to help strengthen our faith in Him in the present for whatever we are facing.

The next challenge for Joshua and the Israelites on their way to the Promised Land was Jericho itself.

Now Jericho was securely shut up because of the
children of Israel; none went out, and none came
in. And the LORD said to Joshua: "See! I have given
Jericho into your hand, its king, and the mighty
men of valor. You shall march around the city, all
you men of war; you shall go all around the city
once. This you shall do six days. And seven priests
shall bear seven trumpets of rams' horns before the
ark. But the seventh day you shall march around

the city seven times, and the priests shall blow the
trumpets. It shall come to pass, when they make a
long blast with the ram's horn, and when you hear
the sound of the trumpet, that all the people shall
shout with a great shout; then the wall of the city
will fall down flat. And the people shall go up every
man straight before him."
(Josh. 6:1–5)

This would appear to be a most unconventional warfare strategy, for all the men of war to march around the city! Not only once, but for six consecutive days? In addition to the men of war, seven priests, bearing seven trumpets and the Ark of the Covenant were to march with them once a day for six days. On the seventh day, God told Joshua to command them to march around the city seven times, and then the priests were to blow the trumpets. The rest of the Israelites were instructed to shout with a great shout, at the top of their lungs, when they heard the trumpets. God told Joshua that when they shouted, the walls of the city would **fall down flat.** The city's protection would be gone, and the Israelites would walk right in and conquer it.

Oh, clap your hands, all you peoples!
Shout to God with the voice of triumph!
For the LORD Most High is awesome;
He is a great King over all the earth.
(Ps. 47:1–2)

Shouting is associated with victory. Football fans shout when their team scores the winning touchdown. With the Israelites and Jericho, however, they were commanded to shout before the walls came down, before they had the victory. This takes great faith in God, "who gives us the victory through our Lord Jesus Christ" (1 Cor. 15:57). Whatever we are facing, whatever walls need to come down in our lives, we can shout in faith the victory that has already been won for us.

2 Corinthians 10:3–4 says, "For though we walk in the flesh, we do not war according to the flesh. For the weapons of our warfare are not carnal but mighty in God for pulling down strongholds." A primary weapon God has given us is faith in God. Hebrews 11:1 says, "Now faith is the substance of things hoped for, the evidence of things not seen." So, when we are confronted with a wall of resistance, whether it be depression, fear, anxiety, or pain, we can shout in faith (in God) with a shout of triumph that God will bring down that wall. We can walk right in and take authority over it. First Thessalonians 4:16 says that the Lord Himself will come down from heaven, how? With a shout—a shout of victory—and the dead in Christ shall rise first. Verse 17 goes on to say, "Then we who are alive and remain shall be caught up together with them in the clouds to meet the Lord in the air. And thus we shall always be with the Lord." Caught up, lifted, taken out of this troubled world into a world where we will never again be troubled by pain, or

sorrow, or tragedy, or death. Now that's worth shouting about!

In Joshua 6:17, Joshua commanded the people to march around the city walls. So they did, once a day for six days, during which the priests continually blew the trumpets and the Ark of the Covenant (which was the presence of the Lord) followed them. The priests ushered in the presence of the Lord, who would give them the victory. First Thessalonians 4:16 goes on to say that not only will the Lord descend from heaven with a shout, but with the trumpet of God. If you've ever watched the Kentucky Derby, you know that it always begins with the sound of a trumpet alerting the attendees that the race is about to begin. The continual blowing of the trumpets by the priests alerted the Israelites and their enemy that the conquest of Jericho was about to begin.

> *But it came to pass on the seventh day that*
> *they rose early, about the dawning of the day,*
> *and marched around the city seven times in the*
> *same manner. On that day only they marched*
> *around the city seven times. And the seventh time*
> *it happened, when the priests blew the trumpets,*
> *that Joshua said to the people: "Shout,*
> *for the Lord has given you the city!"*
> (Josh. 6:15–16)

The word shout in the Hebrew is *truw`ah* (ter-oo-aw›)[34] which means to sound the alarm of war, a battle cry, the shout of the joy of victory. This is another weapon God has given us in our battle with our enemies of pain, worry, anxiety, depression, fear, and trouble. We don't have to take it lying down. We can get up and shout to God with the voice of triumph. The cross of Calvary assures us of the triumph, and the Holy Spirit enables the application of it.

Joshua 6:20 says, "So the people shouted when the priests blew the trumpets. And it happened when the people heard the sound of the trumpet, and the people shouted with a great shout, that the wall fell down flat. Then the people went up into the city, every man straight before him, and they took the city." The people shouted with a great shout, and the walls of the enemy fell down flat. Shouting is not only associated with the victory we have through our Lord Jesus Christ, but also the praise and worship of the One who obtained that victory for us. And so, praise and worship of the King of Kings and Lord of Lords is a primary weapon of our warfare against our enemies alluded to previously. Isaiah 61:3 says in part that the Lord has given us a "garment of praise for the spirit of heaviness." We often call the "spirit of heaviness" *depression*. Praise is a weapon we can use to fight against depression. Consider Psalm 13, which is a good example of a strategy for dealing with depression:

---

[34] Strong, James. "8643 תְּרוּעָה (*ter-oo-aw'*)," Strong's Hebrew: 8643. 8643 תְּרוּעָה (*ter-oo-aw'*) (Strong's Concordance, 2025), https://strongsconcordance.org/

How long, O LORD? Will You forget me forever?
How long will You hide Your face from me?
How long shall I take counsel in my soul,
Having sorrow in my heart daily?
How long will my enemy be exalted over me?

Consider and hear me, O LORD my God;
Enlighten my eyes,
Lest I sleep the sleep of death;
Lest my enemy say,
"I have prevailed against him";
Lest those who trouble me rejoice when I am
moved.

But I have trusted in Your mercy;
My heart shall rejoice in Your salvation.
I will sing to the LORD,
Because He has dealt bountifully with me.

David poured out his heaviness honestly to God and then poured out his praise to God, and God received them both.

There is a pouring out so that there could be a pouring in. Some of us need to understand that it's OK to pour out your complaint and pain and distress to God instead of just holding it all in, keeping it all bottled up. I am one of those.

On December 3, 1975, after the birth of our second son, we were involved in a violent automobile accident on our way to taking him to his first post-delivery checkup. I was driving, my wife was in the front passenger seat holding our baby, and our firstborn toddler son was in the back seat. Upon impact, my wife and I were both knocked unconscious, and our baby dislodged from my wife's arms, hitting his head against the dashboard and rolling under the front seat. After removing me, my wife, and our older son from the vehicle, rescue workers prepared to tow the car away when they suddenly heard the whimpering sound of our baby whom they did not realize had rolled under the seat. They would've towed the car away with our baby still in it had they not heard his whimpering. Our older son was not hurt. My wife and I both suffered concussions, and our baby suffered head trauma. My wife and I were discharged from the hospital after several days, but our baby remained hospitalized for sixteen days. When we brought him home, all he did was vomit and cry, and we had to take him back to the hospital. At this time, medical experts diagnosed him with acquired hydrocephalus from the accident.

Doctors determined that he would need surgery to implant a ventricular shunt in his cranial cavity to relieve the pressure from the buildup of spinal fluid. The surgery was not successful, and so they decided to do a second surgery. After four and a half weeks, they sent us home with our baby still crying and vomiting. All during this time I was trying to stay positive and believe God, which is fine, except for the fact that I was crushed and dying inside. However, I thought I would be unfaithful if I confessed that, so I just bottled it up. Upon discharge from the hospital, our baby was crying and vomiting, my wife was sick, and our older son was also sick. I had to get medication for our older son on our way home. When I came out of the drug store with that medication, I broke. I lost it and yelled out at the top of my lungs to the Lord, "How much do you think I can take? I can't take anymore." At this point, I thought I had lost my salvation and my relationship with the Lord.

However, it was quite the contrary. At that very moment, the Lord spoke to me clearly. "What took you so long to tell me that? I've known you felt that way all along. What made you think you couldn't tell me that?" It was a liberating moment for me. I couldn't change what was happening on the outside, but God could relieve me of what was happening to me on the inside. God was waiting for me to pour that out to Him so that He could pour His comfort into me.

The Result? The wall and the weight of the burden came down with a shout of praise and gratitude, clearing the way forward toward the promised land. For us at that time, the promised land was a renowned pediatric neurosurgeon at Children's Hospital in Philadelphia, who finally fixed our baby—no more crying, no more vomiting. For the Israelites, the walls of Jericho came down, clearing the way for their journey into the Promised Land, Canaan. And ultimately, for all of us who pursue Him, the result will be life forever with the King of Kings and Lord of Lords, Jesus Christ, on the new earth under the new heavens. There will be no more tears, or crying, or sorrow, or pain, and no more death!

Chapter Six

The Reunion

The Man from Heaven

> *There was a man sent from God, whose name*
> *was John. This man came for a witness,*
> *to bear witness of the Light, that all through him*
> *might believe. He was not that Light, but was sent*
> *to bear witness of that Light. That was the true*
> *Light which gives light to every man coming*
> *into the world.*
> (John 1:6–9)

Here we see God starting with light again. Not the light of the sun, or the moon, or the stars, but the light of revelation—the revealing of the Son of God, who was, as Hebrews 1:3 says, "the radiance of God's glory and the *exact* representation of his being" (NIV, emphasis added). The Lord Jesus, Himself, said in John 14:9, "He who has seen Me has seen the Father."

Furthermore, John1:3 says, "All things were made through Him, and without Him nothing was made that was made." So we see that everything was mediated through the Son of God, Jesus. Everything goes through the Son—not the sun. There is no salvation without the Son; there is no eternal life apart from his glorious presence. Without the Son, we are forever separated from the light of His presence and cast into eternal darkness.

God is speaking again as He did at the very beginning of creation. As it says in Hebrews 1:2, "[God] has in these last days spoken to us by His Son, whom He has appointed heir of all things, through whom also He made the worlds." He's spoken to us by his Son, through his Son, Jesus. Again, it was through the Son that God made the worlds. The word "worlds" can be translated "ages."[35] Jesus is the Man, the Mediator of the ages of all time, bringing heaven back to earth, man back to God, and humanity back from the dead, together again. Heaven had come to earth. This one Man was the embodiment of heaven and earth. This one Man manifested the words and works of heaven. Ultimately, this one Man would be the Mediator to bring all of heaven back to a new earth under new heavens. John 1:14 says that the Word, Jesus, became flesh and was made visible. In John 8:12, the Lord Jesus Himself says, "I am the light of the world. He who follows Me shall not walk in darkness, but have the light of life."

Here again, as it was in the beginning, God is saying through his Son, "Let there be light" in this dark world,

---

[35] Jack W. Hayford et al., *New Spirit-Filled Life Bible: New International Version* (Nashville: Thomas Nelson, 2015).

darkened by the prince of darkness. Let there be the revelation of the God of all creation. First John 1:5 says, "This is the message which we have heard from [Jesus] and declare to you, that God is light and in Him is no darkness *at all*" (emphasis added).

The Greek word for darkness is *skotia* (skot-ee›-ah),[36] meaning gloom, evil, ignorance, a lack of spiritual perception and divine truth. Isaiah 60:1 says, "Arise, shine; for your light has come! And the glory of the LORD is risen upon you." I believe this is one of the many Old Testament references to the true light, the true revelation and glory of the God of all creation who was to come into the world, the Lord Jesus.

The glory of the Lord has risen upon **you**—this is referring to the Israelites, the people of God. Again, another prophetic declaration of what was to come. The Lord Jesus said to His disciples, His followers, those who gave up everything to follow Him, "You are the light of the world" (Matt. 5:14). We who are followers of Jesus are to have the same light, the same revelation of the God of all creation, to the world around us. We are reflectors of the light of His glory. What an awesome privilege; what an awesome honor!

If we go back to Genesis 1:14–18, we see that when God said, "Let there be light," He wasn't speaking of the physical heavenly luminaries (i.e. the sun, moon, and stars). He was

---

[36] Strong, James. "4653 σκοτία (*skot-ee'-ah*)" Strong's Greek: 4653. σκοτία (*skot-ee'-ah*) (Strong's Concordance, 2025), https://strongsconcordance.org/

speaking of the revelation, the light of His presence invading the spiritual darkness of the earth. As physical darkness is the absence of light, spiritual darkness is the absence of God's presence. Genesis 1:4 says that God separated the light from the darkness, and verse five says that he called the light day and the darkness night.

However, let's now look at Genesis 1:14–17:

> *Then God said, "Let there be lights in the firmament of the heavens to divide the day from the night; and let them be for signs and seasons, and for days and years; and let them be for lights in the firmament of the heavens to give light on the earth"; and it was so. Then God made two great lights: the greater light to rule the day, and the lesser light to rule the night. He made the stars also. God set them in the firmament of the heavens to give light on the earth.*

Here we see God speaking into existence the sun, moon, and stars to give light to the earth, after He said, "Let there be light" in verse three. So, we may assume that initially He was speaking of light in spiritual terms. The light of His presence separated light from darkness, just as heaven is separated from hell. Heaven is the place of the never-ending light of the presence of the Lord and the glory, peace, and joy that His presence provides. Revelation 22:5, speaking of the new Jerusalem on the new Earth, under the new heavens, says that there will be no night there, no darkness there, and the inhabitants will not need any candles or flashlights or any kind of electrical illumination or sunlight because the Lord God gives them light . Hell, on the other hand, is the place of the never-ending presence of the darkness. This darkness breeds the gloom, sorrow, and horror of the prince of darkness, the devil.

Jesus told a story of a rich man and a beggar named Lazarus.

> *"There was a certain rich man who was clothed in purple and fine linen and fared sumptuously every day. But there was a certain beggar named Lazarus, full of sores, who was laid at his gate, desiring to be fed with the crumbs which fell from the rich man's table. Moreover the dogs came and licked his sores. So it was that the beggar died, and was carried by the angels to Abraham's bosom. The rich man also died and was buried. And being in torments in Hades, he lifted up his eyes and saw Abraham afar off, and Lazarus in his bosom.*

> *"Then he cried and said, 'Father Abraham, have mercy on me, and send Lazarus that he may dip the tip of his finger in water and cool my tongue; for I am tormented in this flame.' But Abraham said, 'Son, remember that in your lifetime you received your good things, and likewise Lazarus evil things; but now he is comforted and you are*

tormented. And besides all this, between us and you there is a great gulf fixed, so that those who want to pass from here to you cannot, nor can those from there pass to us.'"
(Luke 16:19–26)

Can you imagine not only the never-ending torment of hell, but the never-ending torment of being able to see what he missed. He could see it, but he would never taste it. God forbid that should ever be the case for any of us, especially given the fact that we have a Mediator who was willing to mediate our forgiveness through His death on the cross. He was willing to taste the death of eternal separation from the Father so we would **never** have to taste it. "Jesus cried out with a loud voice, saying, 'Eloi, Eloi, lama sabachthani?' which is translated, 'My God, My God, why have You forsaken Me?'" (Mark 15:34)

This reminds me of a family trip we took many years ago to San Francisco. During that trip, we visited Alcatraz. We were able to purchase earphones and listen to commentary from former guards and prisoners of Alcatraz. I will never forget when one prisoner expressed great anguish over the fact that every New Year's Eve, he could hear from the barred windows of the prison everyone celebrating the new year. He could hear it, but he couldn't have it.

But concerning the times and the seasons, brethren, you have no need that I should write to you. For you yourselves know perfectly that the

day of the Lord so comes as a thief in the night.
For when they say, "Peace and safety!" then
sudden destruction comes upon them, as labor
pains upon a pregnant woman. And they shall not
escape. But you, brethren, are not in darkness, so
that this Day should overtake you as a thief. You
are all sons of light and sons of the day. We are
not of the night nor of darkness.
(1 Thess. 5:1–5).

Sons and daughters of light, sons and daughters of the day. This is not speaking of natural light, but spiritual enlightenment. Spiritual enlightenment has to do with the revelation of the Lord Jesus, through whom we have life—a life that never ends. A life that will never have pain, or sickness, or tears, or sorrow, or fear, or worry. No more death! The apostle John says of the Lord Jesus, "In Him was life, and the life was the light of men" (1:4) The life was the light because it was the life of the eternal God. That was the life that was in the Lord Jesus. It was the same life that God breathed into Adam at his creation, and into Eve when she was made from Adam. Tragically, they lost that life through the deception of the serpent. The light and life of the eternal God went out. It was that light that Jesus came to turn back on. It was that life that Jesus came to put back into us. In John 20:22 it says that Jesus breathed on his disciples and said to them, "Receive the Holy Spirit."

God breathed the same breath into Adam, the breath of the eternal life of the eternal God.

As mentioned earlier, John 8:12 says we shall not walk in darkness. Walking in darkness would mean not having the enlightenment of the will and ways of God. Walking in darkness would mean working and living according to the dictates of our fleshly desires, inspired by the same one who deceived Adam and Eve into doing likewise and brought them under his control. This shall_not be the case for us, because Jesus came into the world to bring back the light— the revelation of God and His ways. More personally, He came to bring that enlightenment into my world and your world. When His light comes into my world, then I become like Him, "the light of the world," as He says in Matthew 5:14. This is evidenced by how we speak and live and love— how we conduct ourselves in the world around us just as Jesus did.

The Lord Jesus, our Mediator, the Light of the World, brought heaven back to earth. I call this the reunion, heaven coming back to earth in the form of a Man, as we said previously. The Lord Jesus was the embodiment of heaven and earth. Son of Man and Son of God in one body bringing heaven back to earth, man back to God, and mankind back to mankind.

How was this to be accomplished? How would this Man from heaven, the Son of God, accomplish this?

Let's go back to the Old Testament, 1 Kings chapter 6, where Solomon is building the temple for a dwelling place for the presence of the Lord. Verse 23 speaks of cherubim (heavenly angelic beings) carved out of olive wood. Verse 27 says that two of them were set inside the inner house with wings spans that went from one wall to another. Verse 29 says that all of the walls of the temple were covered with cherubim, palm trees, and open flowers all made of olive wood. Verse 31 says that the doors to the entrance of the sanctuary, where the presence of the Lord would dwell, were made of olive wood. What is the significance of the olive wood, and what is God saying?

Olive wood is dense, heavy, and durable, speaking of permanence. It is also the sign of peace between God and man. You may remember that during the great flood Noah sent out a dove from the ark to see if the floodwaters had receded. The dove came back to the ark with an olive leaf in its mouth, signifying the restoration of peace upon the earth. This was just one of many foreshadowings pointing to the Mediator who would negotiate true and lasting peace for the inhabitants of earth. In Luke 2:14, the angels proclaimed to the shepherds the coming of the Lord Jesus saying, "Glory to God in the highest, and on earth peace, goodwill toward men!" Research indicates that the inscription on the cross which referred to Jesus as the King of the Jews was written on an olive leaf. Archaeological findings further suggest that the cross upon which the Lord Jesus was crucified was made of olive wood.[37]

---

[37] Jack W. Hayford et al., *New Spirit-Filled Life Bible: New International Version* (Nashville: Thomas Nelson, 2015).

The Lord Jesus went into the garden of Gethsemane to pray. He poured out His soul to the Father before He went to the cross. He knew the enormity of what He was facing, and to say it was heavy upon Him is a gross understatement.

> *Then He said to them, "My soul is exceedingly sorrowful, even to death. Stay here and watch."*
>
> *He went a little farther, and fell on the ground, and prayed that if it were possible, the hour might pass from Him. And He said, "Abba, Father, all things are possible for You. Take this cup away from Me; nevertheless, not what I will, but what You will."*
> (Mark 14:34–36)

Have you ever been in such a situation? Have you ever come face-to-face with the death of a loved one, and agonized over it as the Lord Jesus did? The Lord Jesus says to the Father, "*All* things are possible for You. Take this cup away from Me" (emphasis added). However, the Father didn't take it from Him. He went to the cross. He had to die. In Matthew 19:26, Jesus says that "with God all things are possible." God doesn't always do what He's able to do. There isn't anything He can't do. There isn't anything too hard for Him. He is omnipotent. We know He **can** do it, but what **will** He do?

The Lord Jesus is saying to his Father, "Take this cup (of death) away from Me." Remember, He was not only the Son of God, He was also the Son of Man. He was human and had human feelings. He was able to experience the agony of His humanity, just like us. Hebrews 4:15 says that we don't have a High Priest, speaking of the Lord Jesus, who can't be touched with what touches us. How did the Lord Jesus settle it? "Nevertheless, not what I will, but what You will [be done]" (Mark 14:36).

This is a major issue among us. I've heard people say, "If God is a healer, why doesn't everyone get healed?" I believe that yes, God is a healer, and yet, He alone reserves the right to heal whom He **will**, and no one can dictate to Him otherwise. If anyone does, they put themselves in the place of God, and no one can ever do that. He alone is God, and there is none other. Ecclesiastes 3:1 says, "To everything [healing, living, dying] there is a season, a time for every purpose under heaven." What did Jesus teach His disciples to pray? "Your will be done on earth as it is in heaven" (Matt. 6:10). If heaven has determined that I should be healed and given me the faith for it, I shall be healed. If heaven is determined to call me home, I am going home! Nevertheless, not my will, but Thy will be done. That's how we settle it.

Gethsemane means "oil press,"[38] which most likely means it was an olive garden, which included a press for crushing oil from the olives. It was not merely coincidence that the Lord Jesus went to this garden with His three disciples. He knew

---

[38] Strong, James. "1068 Γεθσημανῆ (*gheth-say-man-ay'*)" Strong's Greek: 1968. Γεθσημανῆ (*gheth-say-man-ay'*) (Strong's Concordance, 2025), https://strongsconcordance.org/

this was how He was going to obtain our peace with the Father as Isaiah prophesied in chapter 53 and verse five in the New International Version, "He was crushed for our iniquities." That crushing began in an olive garden, where He began to be pressed with the weight of the sin of the world upon Him. Luke 22:44 says that he was in such great agony that "His sweat became like great drops of blood falling down to the ground."

He was then crushed on an olive tree, which (as noted earlier) is a dense, heavy, durable wood suggesting permanence. The Lord Jesus would obtain for us a lasting, permanent place in heaven by virtue of His death on the olive tree. Romans 5:1 says that having been justified, cleared of all charges, declared righteous, we have peace with God. How? By the Lord Jesus's willingness to be crushed for our sin instead of allowing us to be crushed for it. If we had to be crushed for it, we would never recover. We would be cast into outer darkness, where there is "weeping and gnashing of teeth," as it says in Matthew 8:12. "Gnashing of teeth" in the Greek suggests extreme anguish and utter despair of the condemned to eternal punishment.[39] Can you imagine being punished forever? Can you imagine being in extreme anguish and utter despair that never ends? That's the condemnation that Jesus saved us from, as it says in Romans 8:1, "There is therefore, *now* no condemnation to those who are in Christ Jesus" (emphasis added).

---

[39] Jack W. Hayford et al., *New Spirit-Filled Life Bible: New International Version* (Nashville: Thomas Nelson, 2015).

Here was another Tree of Life the Father was providing for us—the olive wood cross upon which Jesus gave His life for the sin of the inhabited world.

> *"Abide in Me, and I in you. As the branch cannot bear fruit of itself, unless it abides in the vine, neither can you, unless you abide in Me.*
>
> *"I am the vine, you are the branches. He who abides in Me, and I in him, bears much fruit; for without Me you can do nothing."*
> (John 15:4–5)

The branch cannot bear fruit of itself, separated from the vine. The Man from heaven, the Mediator, used His own body and blood to negotiate reconnection to the heavenly vine that gives life-bearing fruit of the Spirit as described in Galatians 5:22–23. We cannot bear fruit apart from Him, the life-giving vine. Again, the Lord Jesus says in John 15:5, "Without Me you can do nothing." You are unfruitful and dried up.

Jesus says in John 10:10, "I have come that they may have life, and that they may have it more abundantly." What is the implication of that statement? The life we have apart from Him is going to end up forever separated from Him, the source of life. He is the source of love, joy, and peace that never ends. That's why the Lord Jesus says, "I have come." He had to come. He could not bear the thought of us being forever separated from Him and cast into a hellish torment forever. His love for us compelled Him to come.

His love for you and me enabled Him to endure the cross, despising the shame of it, which could've deterred Him. We often see pictures of the Lord Jesus hanging on the cross with a loin cloth around his waist. However, historians tell us that was not the case; there was no loin cloth. He bore the same shame of the first man, Adam and his wife Eve who sinned by eating of the forbidden fruit of the tree of the knowledge of good and evil. Their eyes were opened when they ate of it, and they saw that they were naked and were ashamed. Because of "the joy that was set before Him," He endured it all (Heb. 12:2). What was that joy? That whoever believes on Him would not be tormented forever but have everlasting life with Him (John 3:16).

2 Peter 3:9 says, "The Lord is not slack concerning His promise, as some count slackness, but is longsuffering toward us, not willing that any should perish but that all should come to repentance." The Greek word for repentance is *metanoia* (met-an'-oy-ah).[40] It means to have a change of mind that leads to a change of action and direction. I was headed in the direction of death, but now the Mediator has come to mediate a change of mind and turn me back around in the direction that leads to everlasting life.

1 Corinthians 15:22 says, "For as in Adam all die, even so in Christ all shall be made alive." We were all born with the Adamic nature, which was destined for death because of its separation from the life of God through sin. First

---

[40] Strong, James. "3341 μετάνοια (*met-an'-oy-ah*)" Strong's Greek: 3341. μετάνοια (*met-an'-oy-ah*) (Strong's Concordance, 2025), https://strongsconcordance.org/

Corinthians 15:26 goes on to say that the last enemy to be destroyed is death. Our ultimate enemy is not the devil, it is death, and our adversary, the devil, knows that.

We are not talking about physical death here. We are talking about spiritual death, which is eternal separation from God, the Author of Life. Luke 12:4 says that we who belong to Christ should not fear physical death, because after that there is no more that can be done to us. In fact, after our physical death, we will live in eternal bliss in the glorious presence of Christ. Luke 12:5 then goes on to let us know whom we should fear. "Fear Him who, after He has killed, has power to cast into hell." How does God kill us? By banishing to hell those who have rejected the salvation of his Son. He is the one we should fear in the sense of having a healthy respect and reverence for Him. He has the power to do it, but He sent his only begotten Son to take our place so He wouldn't have to cast us into hell. Ezekiel 33:11 says that God takes no pleasure in the death of the wicked; it grieves Him. First John 2:23 says, "He who acknowledges the Son has the Father also." The word acknowledges in the Greek means to confess, not to refuse, to declare openly, to profess oneself the worshiper of one, to praise, celebrate, to come into agreement (with God).[41]

First Corinthians 15:55 says, "O Death, where is your sting? O Hades, where is your victory?" This is the fulfillment of Hosea 13:14 in the Old Testament, which says, "I will

[41] Jack W. Hayford et al., *New Spirit-Filled Life Bible: New International Version* (Nashville: Thomas Nelson, 2015).

deliver this people from the power of the grave; I will redeem them from death. Where, O death, are your plagues? Where, O grave, is your destruction?" (NIV). The Lord Jesus released us from the penalty of spiritual death, eternal separation from God, and the power of an everlasting hell. He was willing, as Hebrews 2:9 says, to taste death for each of us. He cried out from the cross "Eloi, Eloi, lama sabachthani," which means "My God, my God, why have You forsaken me?"[42] Why did God forsake His Son? For our sakes, so that we would never have to cry out those words. Thank God that Jesus only "tasted" death so that He could take it into the tomb and leave it there upon his resurrection. Death no longer had power over Him or over those who put their trust in Him. Hallelujah!

All of this will culminate in the grand finale described in the revelation the apostle John had on the isle of Patmos. John had been banished to Patmos for his faith in Christ Jesus, after authorities unsuccessfully attempted to kill him in a cauldron of boiling hot oil.[43]

Now I saw a new heaven and a new earth, for the first heaven and the first earth had passed away. Also there was no more sea. Then I, John, saw the holy city, New Jerusalem, coming down out of heaven from God, prepared as a bride adorned

[42] Jack W. Hayford et al., *New Spirit-Filled Life Bible: New International Version* (Nashville: Thomas Nelson, 2015).

[43] Jack W. Hayford et al., *New Spirit-Filled Life Bible: New International Version* (Nashville: Thomas Nelson, 2015).

for her husband. And I heard a loud voice from heaven saying, "Behold, the tabernacle of God is with men, and He will dwell with them, and they shall be His people. God Himself will be with them and be their God. And God will wipe away every tear from their eyes; there shall be no more death, nor sorrow, nor crying. There shall be no more pain, for the former things have passed away."

Then He who sat on the throne said, "Behold, I make all things new." And He said to me, "Write, for these words are true and faithful."

And He said to me, "It is done! I am the Alpha and the Omega, the Beginning and the End. I will give of the fountain of the water of life freely to him who thirsts. He who overcomes shall inherit all things, and I will be his God and he shall be My son. But the cowardly, unbelieving, abominable, murderers, sexually immoral, sorcerers, idolaters, and all liars shall have their part in the lake which burns with fire and brimstone, which is the second death."
(Rev. 21:1–8)

The apostle John saw a new heaven, which refers to the sky and the regions above the earth. This could possibly suggest a new atmosphere—new air to breathe, which the Prince of the Power of the Air could no longer pollute with demonic spiritual influences. No more, as Ephesians 6:12 says, "principalities, powers, rulers of the darkness of this age, and spiritual hosts of wickedness in the heavenly places." There will be new heavenly places with hosts of righteousness, holiness, goodness, love, joy, and everlasting peace. As He says in verse five, "Behold, I make all things new."

There will also be a new earth, the purpose of which shall be a dwelling place to be inhabited by those who have been made new after the likeness of God's Son. Those who have been made clean, made fit for habitation with the Lamb of God and God Himself.

The apostle John says in Revelation 21:1 that he saw that there was no more sea. This was one of several things that God said would be no more. The sea, the night, the sun, the moon, and the temple.

We might wonder why there would be no more sea. Revelation 20:13 says that "the sea gave up the dead who were in it." A Hebrew word for sea is *yam* (yawm),[44] which means a body of water, but with the underlying suggestion of a roaring body of water. A roaring body of water spells danger. How much death and devastation have been caused by roaring bodies of water?

There will be no night there, as we said previously speaking of illumination, and no darkness, as it says in Revelation 21:25 and 22:5, referring to the darkness of evil. The devil himself is often referred to as the Prince

---

[44] Strong, James. "3220 יָם (*yawm*)," Strong's Hebrew: 3220. יָם (*yawm*) (Strong's Concordance, 2025), https://strongsconcordance.org/

of Darkness, suggesting he is the originator of darkness. Darkness is reserved for the inhabitants of hell who tragically rejected faith in the Son of God to save them from such eternal darkness. Darkness also speaks of darkened behavior and shameful deeds, done in secret. There will be none of that on the new earth, because there will be no darkness there. There will be nothing hidden there. The light of the glory of God will bring exposure, and only those who can stand the exposure of the light will be there. First Corinthians 6:9–10 says in essence that the unrighteous, fornicators (those who indulge in sex outside of marriage), idolaters (worshipers of someone or something above God), adulterers, homosexuals, sodomites (male homosexuals), thieves, covetous (greedy), drunkards, revilers, or extortioners will not be on the new earth.

In Acts 26:18, the apostle Paul recounted his revelation of the Lord Jesus and conversion to Christianity on the road to Damascus. Ironically, he was on his way to Damascus to kill more Christians considered to be blasphemers of God. However, now that he had become one of the very ones he sought to kill, Jesus let him know that He was going to use him to turn people from darkness to light, and from the power of Satan to the power of God.

The Lord Jesus says in John 3:20, "Everyone practicing evil hates the light." In the new Jerusalem, there will be no night there, no darkness of evil, no haters of the light.

First Thessalonians 5:5 says that we, lovers of God through Christ Jesus our Lord and Savior, are children of light. We walk and live in the light of the truth of God's word. We are children of the day, not the darkness of the night. We love the Light, personified in the Lord Jesus, the Light of the World. He is the forgiving and cleansing Light who sets us free from our captivity to the darkness of evil and all that is not right in our lives.

As we said previously, there was no more sea. In addition to the sea being the cause of death, it also separated the lands and peoples from one another. There will be no more of such separation and division of peoples from and against each other. In Revelation 7:9, the apostle John describes his vision of a great multitude of all nations, tribes, tongues, and peoples standing before the throne of the Lamb.

The only body of water that will be on the newly formed earth will be the one spoken of in Revelation 22:1, "He showed me a pure river of water of life, clear as crystal, proceeding from the throne of God and of the Lamb." Pure, clear as crystal, uncontaminated, unpolluted, straight from the very throne of God. No more undrinkable saltwater, no more droughts, and no more floods, always the perfect water level.

Revelation 21:2 says, "Then I, John, saw the holy city, New Jerusalem, coming down out of heaven from God, prepared as a bride adorned for her husband." Here we finally see heaven and earth coming back together again. In the beginning, God prepared a garden to live in with Adam and Eve. Here we see it is a city, the new Jerusalem, where the Lamb, the King of Kings and Lord of Lords, shall live together with His bride who has been prepared just for Him.

When you think of a city, you think of people or "citizens." What is a city without citizens? A ghost town. The new Jerusalem won't be a ghost town, but it will be a "Holy Ghost Town." The Holy Spirit will emanate from the Lamb and forever rest upon and live in the citizens of the New Jerusalem.

> *I heard a loud voice from heaven saying, "Behold, the tabernacle of God is with men, and He will dwell with them, and they shall be His people. God Himself will be with them and be their God.*
> (Rev. 21:3)

A loud voice. What is one thing you think of when you hear a loud voice? A voice that demands your attention. A voice that must be heard. Now hear this: God is back! He has come down from heaven to dwell upon the new earth He created for people that have been re-created in the image and likeness of His Son, who is the image and likeness of the invisible God.

This time, there will be no serpent allowed upon this new earth. He will have been cast into the lake of fire, along with all of those who have refused the forgiveness of their sins that forever separated them from the God of heaven. The citizens of the New Jerusalem have already settled that, as it says in Rev. 12:11, "And they overcame him by the blood of the Lamb and by the word of their testimony, and they did not love their lives to the death." And many did die for their testimony of Jesus. We may not literally die for our testimony of Jesus, but we will die to our will and our way, and to the will and way of others, for the sake of His will and His way.

God has brought it all the way back to the beginning. It is going to end the way it began—God living together with His people forever. He will be **their** God, and they will be **His** people. A people who have been cleansed and made righteous with the blood of the Lamb. Second Timothy 2:19 says, "The Lord knows those who are His." We can't fool God. He knows those who are His.

> *"Not everyone who says to Me, 'Lord, Lord,' shall enter the kingdom of heaven, but he who does the will of My Father in heaven. Many will say to Me in that day, 'Lord, Lord, have we not prophesied in Your name, cast out demons in Your name, and done many wonders in Your name?' And then I will declare to them, 'I never knew you; depart from Me, you who practice lawlessness!'"*
> (Matt. 7:21–23)

What is the distinction between those who are His and those who are not? Those who are all talk, and those who live it out. But the Lord Jesus goes on to make the further distinction between those who **do** according to **His** will, and for **His** glory, and those who **do** prophesy, cast out demons, and many wonders according to **their** will, and for **their own** glory.

The Lord Jesus says to them, "I never knew you, depart from Me, you who practice lawlessness." That word in the

Greek means to be without law; an outlaw.[45] Some may look like they are working for God and with God, having as second Timothy 3:5 says, "a form of godliness," but denying His authoritative power over them. God knows our heart. He knows those who are truly for Him and with Him in heart because they live under His rule, and according to His will.

This is the reward of the righteous: the unbroken fellowship, friendship, and communion with our ever-loving God and Father and his beloved Son, Jesus.

Revelation 21:4 says, "And God will wipe away every tear from their eyes; there shall be no more death, nor sorrow, nor crying. There shall be no more pain, for the former things have passed away." God will wipe away every memory that made us cry. There will never be any crying again, or sorrow, or pain, and no more death to separate us from one another. For the former things that caused crying, and sorrow, and pain, and death will themselves pass away and be no more. Think about that! Let that sink down deep into your spirit whenever you feel sad. Know that a day is coming when these things, and the memory of them, shall be no more—as though they never happened, never again. It will be as it was in the beginning with Adam and Eve, who knew only God before their ill-fated decision to know evil.

In Revelation 21:5, God says, "Behold, I make all things new," and we might add "for all those who have been made a new creation in Christ Jesus," as it says in

---

[45] Jack W. Hayford et al., *New Spirit-Filled Life Bible: New International Version* (Nashville: Thomas Nelson, 2015).

Second Corinthians 5:17. The work that has been done on the inside will now be done on the outside. There will be a coming together again. No longer will it be new people living in an old world. It will be new people living in a new world, inhabited by heaven itself and the Lord of heaven Himself!

In Revelation 21:6, God says to the apostle John, "It is done! I am the Alpha and Omega, the Beginning and the End." God started it, and He will finish it after a long detour in between. Have you ever wondered why such a long detour, and what delays His coming? Galatians 4:4 says, "When the fullness of the time had come, God sent forth his Son." It's a matter of God's appointed time, and the fullness of it, giving everyone, everywhere time to hear the gospel of his Son and time to respond affirmatively. As mentioned earlier, 2 Peter 3:9 says that God desires all to come to repentance. As far as heaven is concerned, it is already finished, but it is not yet finished on earth.

"I am the Alpha and the Omega, the Beginning and the End, the First and the Last."

Blessed are those who do His commandments, that they may have the right to the tree of life, and may enter through the gates into the city. But outside are dogs and sorcerers and sexually immoral and murderers and idolaters, and whoever loves and practices a lie.
(Rev. 22:13–15)

God repeats the fact that life never-ending begins with Him, the great I Am, and ends with Him. And in the end, those that have access, and have the right to enter into the gates, and into the city, the New Jerusalem, are not those who say and not do, but those who do what they say. More specifically, those who do what He says, those who obey His commands. Talk is cheap; action speaks louder than words. What will the Lord Jesus say when we stand before Him? "Well done." He doesn't say, "Well said," but "Well done. You did what I told you to do." And those who do, and not just say, will live forever with the King of Kings and Lord of Lords.

Those who do otherwise will be outside forever, so that all that is not of God shall be separated from Him and so that all that is of God will never be separated from God again.

Heaven will never be separated from earth again. Mankind will never be separated from God again, and death will never separate us from one another again. We will **never** know that grief again. It will truly be heaven on earth. And all because the Mediator, the Lord Jesus, negotiated the reunion with his death on the cross, paying the penalty for our sin that separated heaven from earth, God from us, and us from one another. We will spend all eternity thanking Him for that. If God had not been willing to send his Son into this world, and had the Son not been willing, we would've spent all eternity in an underworld of darkness where there is never ending weeping and sorrow, and anguish and regret. Oh, glory to God in the highest! Praise and thanksgiving be unto the Lamb of God who takes away the sin of the world!

About The Author

*P*astor Jack Rehill is an ordained minister with the Assemblies of God. He earned his Bachelor of Arts in Sociology from Kings College and his Masters of Social Work from Marywood University. He also participated in a post-graduate program in Structural Family Therapy through Philadelphia Child Guidance and is certified as a Structural Family Therapist. He has served as President/CEO of the local subsidary of the Volunteers of America Christian Social Service Agency, serving children, teens, and adults in various therapeutic settings. As a PA-licensed clinical social worker, Jack has worked in the mental health field & Christ directed counseling for over 42 years.

When first saved, coming out of the "hippie" generation of the sixties, Jack desired to go straight into Bible College and ministry. However, the Lord very clearly told him to "stay in his course of study, and He would use me in that field." Many years later, after accepting a position with Volunteers of America, he became a licensed minister. He says, "The Lord showed me that my desire to move into ministry from many years ago was happening."

Outside of his love for ministry, Jack is an avid exercise enthusiast: from racquetball to basketball to weightlifting. Once in a while, he enjoys driving a Sprint Cup race car at Pocono Raceway at speeds of 150 mph.

Jack and his wife Patti were married in August of 1971. They have four children & two granddaughters and more recently, a grandson. Patti has been retired from harvest church as an administrative assistant after 25 years of service. Before Harvest, she earned her degree in nursing and worked in a variety of settings, from hospitals to home health.

Jack and Patti are beach lovers and try to get there as often as they can. They enjoy worship music, both contemporary and some of the old favorites from years past.

They also love to open their home to people to encourage them in their faith in Christ Jesus.

www.ingramcontent.com/pod-product-compliance
Lightning Source LLC
Chambersburg PA
CBHW071744120626
46550CB00002B/656